FIGHTING BACK

STAN ANDREWS
AND THE BIRTH OF
THE ISRAELI AIR FORCE

Jeffrey Weiss and Craig Weiss

WICKED SON

A WICKED SON BOOK
An Imprint of Post Hill Press
ISBN: 978-1-63758-311-1
ISBN (eBook): 978-1-63758-312-8

Fighting Back:
Stan Andrews and the Birth of the Israeli Air Force
© 2022 by Jeffrey Weiss and Craig Weiss
All Rights Reserved

Cover Design by Tiffani Shea

This is a work of nonfiction. All people, locations, events, and situations
are portrayed to the best of the author's memory.

"The Army Air Corps Song"
by Robert Crawford. Courtesy of Carl Fischer, LLC

"San Fernando Valley"
Words and Music by Gordon Jenkins
© 1943 (Renewed) EDWIN H. MORRIS & COMPANY, A Division of MPL
Music Publishing, Inc. All Rights Reserved
Reprinted by Permission of Hal Leonard LLC

"He Wears a Pair of Silver Wings"
Words by Eric Maschwitz
Music by Michael Carr
Copyright (c) 1941 by The Peter Maurice Co., Ltd., London, England
Copyright Renewed and Assigned to Shapiro, Bernstein & Co., Inc., New York
for the U.S.A. and Canada International Copyright Secured All Rights Reserved
Used by Permission
Reprinted by Permission of Hal Leonard LLC

Post Hill Press
New York • Nashville
posthillpress.com

Published in the United States of America
1 2 3 4 5 6 7 8 9 10

For my children Danny, Abby, Tali, and Aaron—who never cease to inspire me and to make me proud to be their father— and to Orlie, who has enriched my life beyond imagining and with whom I am sharing my own Israel adventure. —Jeff

For my wife Erica, who brought the joy of Judaism into my life, and for my children Yoni and Maya, who fill me with hope for the next generation of Jewish heroes. —Craig

Contents

A shkelon is a quiet beach town, some thirty miles south of Tel Aviv. It became part of Israel on November 5, 1948, after the young nation's army succeeded in driving out Egyptian forces during what would become known as the War of Independence.

The town grew slowly during the state's first decades. On its eastern, southern, and northern borders, there was only desert—a barren landscape that brought to mind the surface of the moon. Children who lived near the city's edge would play among the dunes. One spot, in particular, was a favorite site for their games. It was called *Givat HaMatos*—Airplane Hill. No one was sure why.

Over the years, Ashkelon expanded, reclaiming more and more of the surrounding desert. In 1994, a work crew was operating along the edge of town—near *Givat HaMatos*—preparing the area for yet another new neighborhood. Their bulldozer struck metal, something that looked like it might be from a plane, and the air force was called in to identify the remains.

First on the scene was Amit Shrem, a young officer who had an idea about what had been uncovered. He thought it might be from an Israeli bomber that had crash-landed in the Negev more than forty-five years earlier, during one of the climactic battles of the war. There wasn't much left to analyze—a section of wing, parts of a propeller, a portion of the engine cowlings, and other fragments—all long ago stripped clean either by the fire that burned for hours after the plane had ground to a halt in the sand or the subsequent years of exposure to the unforgiving elements. Still, Amit knew what he was looking for, and what he found was enough to confirm his hunch about the plane's identity.

Amit related all of this to Jeff in a phone call in 2009. Jeff was researching that plane, or, more to the point, one of the men who had been on it for its last mission. From the background noise, it was clear that Amit was in the car with one of his kids, but he did not mind the interruption. He described the events of that day in a straightforward, matter-of-fact tone—the phone call to the museum where he was then serving, his trip out to the construction site, and his verification of the plane's identity. But then he shifted. There was one thing, he said, that was *maftia* and *meragesh* (surprising and moving). He told about the excavation of the section of wing. It otherwise had no paint on it, understandable from all it had been through. Yet, as Amit immediately saw, the IAF Jewish Star emblem was still there—somehow, impossibly, intact.

* * *

Craig stood in the small apartment of Libby Anekstein, excited at the prospect of getting some answers to questions that he and Jeff had been struggling with for almost ten years. After exchanging pleasantries, Libby handed Craig a letter written more than sixty years earlier, one that had outlived both the writer and the recipient.

The letter was addressed to Irving "Is" Anekstein, Libby's husband, who had passed away within the last year. It was written by his brother Stan Andrews in April of 1948, only a few short weeks before Stan would travel to Palestine to join a skeleton air force as the local Jews prepared for independence and a certain invasion by the surrounding Arab nations. For nearly a decade, Craig and Jeff had longed to learn more about Stan. Perhaps foremost among their unanswered questions was why Stan had gone to Israel, a decision that was out of character with his entire life to that point.

A few minutes earlier, Craig had asked Libby why she thought Stan had done it. "We don't have to wonder why he went; he told us," she had said as she handed him the letter. Craig began to read, aloud, to Libby and her daughter Narissa, the only other persons present:

"This, in its own little way, is going to be a very momentous letter, so I'd advise you to lean back and prepare yourself. I am leaving Los Angeles this Saturday (the 24th) and shall probably arrive in N.Y. that night. After about two weeks there, spent in obtaining my passport, I shall proceed across to Europe and thence, by various devious and melodramatic routes known only to a favored mysterious few, I go to Palestine. There I shall be engaged in my one-time and unlamented profession, flying combat.

"I don't think it's really necessary to tell you why I am going. Aside from repeating that I don't believe in Zionism any more than you do, I can only say that I feel it's my fight as well as any other Jews, particularly after their betrayal[1] by the U.S. Here is a thing that hundreds of thousands of Jews want, that, by their suffering, they have come to deserve, that is being attacked by Fascists, and that can only be won by fighting, a thing at which I'm fairly adept. I think it's as clear cut as that, but even if it were shadowed by other angles and facets of the situation, I would still go, because it represents to me one of the few chances that a Jew has to fight back against his tormentors and oppressors."

Craig paused and considered the incongruity of a person about to embark on arguably the most extreme of Zionist actions—going to Israel to fight for a Jewish state—declaring a lack of belief in Zionism. Stan was, it was becoming clear, a person whose motivations defied easy explanation. The research journey had reached a critical milestone with the discovery of Stan's letter to his brother and yet, at the same time, it was apparent that it was now only really beginning.

---

[1]   Stan was referring to statements by the U.S. State Department the prior month, suggesting a retreat from prior American support of the partition of Palestine into Jewish and Arab states. In its place, the U.S. was advocating for the creation of a U.N. trusteeship over Palestine, something that would have ended the Zionist dream of an independent Jewish nation.

T he Americans of Stan Andrews' era, those who lived their formative years during the Depression and went off to serve in World War II, have been referred to as the "Greatest Generation." There is an analog to that—the Greatest Jewish Generation. They were the ones who witnessed the largest Jewish tragedy in modern history, the Holocaust, and its claiming of the lives of one-third of all of world Jewry, and who were part of the fight against the forces of evil who were responsible for it. They then took part in the greatest Jewish miracle in modern history—the dramatic birth of the State of Israel in a stirring military victory only three years later, ending two thousand years of exile and putting to rest once and for all the reviled or pitied image of the Wandering Jew. Stan epitomizes the members of this highly select group of no more than a few thousand, his experiences a microcosm of a larger Jewish drama playing out on the international stage: a play in three acts that began with apparent belonging and acceptance in the pre-war world, the shock of anti-Semitism in the war years, and the great Jewish return to Zion after the war.

During our work on this book, we were often asked why we chose to write about Stan. Of course, writing about him meant more than just putting words on a page. Over more than twenty years, it included locating as many people as we could who had been close to him, including a ninety-three-year-old sister, an eighty-five-year-old sister-in-law, former classmates, old friends, and squadron-mates in World War II and Israel. It meant tracking down school yearbooks, a squadron memory book, high school and college essays, war-time letters, short stories written between wars, after-action reports from two wars—not to mention extensive archival research in both English and Hebrew.

From our prior book on Americans in Israel's War of Independence, *I Am My Brother's Keeper*, we got to know many of the stories of the one thousand or so North American volunteers. There were World War II aces, a member of the famed Black Sheep Squadron, the X-1 test pilot before Chuck Yeager, a former escapee from German captivity as a POW, the leading IAF aces of the War of Independence, the first commander of the Israel Navy, and Israel's first general.

There were others who made a greater impact on the course of the war in Israel, some who had more glamorous records from WWII, and several who could lay claim to both things. To be sure, Stan's service in the Israeli Air Force (IAF) during the war was significant, impactful, and unique. He flew combat missions as a member of two different squadrons— the first fighter squadron and a bomber squadron. Between his service in those two squadrons, while holding the rank of major and using an assumed name, he worked with some of Israel's most senior military officials, including a future head of the Mossad, a future chief of staff, and a future prime minister.

Stan, however, was a source of interest for reasons that went far beyond the details of his wartime service in Israel. He was a study in contrasts. In high school during the 1930s, like so many of his classmates at that time, he had been strongly anti-war. Yet, during WWII, he became a talented and aggressive bomber pilot who sought action. For the cause of a Jewish state, he volunteered to return to combat for a second time when other veterans were anxious to make up for the years lost during WWII and build their postwar lives.

He had immense creative talent; he was both an artist and a writer. Stan's art included realistic and abstract works (he was equally comfortable with both) and everything from pencil sketches to oil paintings. Given the depth of his artistic talent, his passion for writing was a surprise. But he longed to be a writer, beginning in high school (from which he graduated at sixteen) and continuing through college (where he graduated at nineteen), World War II, and in the years that followed. His writing proved to be a powerful vehicle for exploring the issues that most moved him at different stages of his life. He was drawn to themes, whether it was the awkward teenage boy looking to find his way with girls, the atheist soldier confronting the possibility of death on the battlefield, the combat pilot losing his nerve, or the assimilated Jew struggling with anti-Semitism. A friend sizing him up in 1948 could have easily imagined him becoming a successful artist, an accomplished writer, or both.

Stan's Judaism was also a study in contrast. He never once set foot in a synagogue before going to Israel, changed his name from the obviously Jewish "Anekstein" to the gentile "Andrews," was embarrassed about his Jewishness (once refusing to admit it to a WWII tentmate who was himself Jewish), and, in 1948, was in a serious relationship with a non-Jewish woman whom he was poised to marry. Yet, he was so aroused by the anti-Semitism of his day that he decided to risk everything to fight so that the Jews could have a state. He was in many ways the quintessential Zionist but at the same time professed to not "give a damn about Zionism."

He was a source of admiration for those around him, yet he was—as John Hersey said of one of his characters in *A Bell for Adano*—"weak in certain attractive, human ways." He was a ladies' man but turned away from the wide-open carousing of postwar Los Angeles to embark on a committed relationship with a tender, thoughtful woman who was determined to marry him. He could be sarcastic in the face of unfairness and had a difficult-to-conceal contempt for those in positions of power, although at the same time, was a devoted friend with a playful sense of humor, which he sometimes expressed in poetry.

Stan epitomized the modern Jew of the years between World War I and II—assimilated, seemingly secure of his place in the modern world, aloof to the point of disdain from organized religious observance, and uninterested in the Zionist dream of restoring Jewish independence in Palestine. As it had for Theodor Herzl some fifty years earlier, anti-Semitism changed everything. While French response to the Dreyfus trial had been the catalyst for Herzl's journey to Zionism, for Stan it was the more mundane anti-Semitism of 1940s America—the "little remarks that you can't poke a guy for, but have to smile and take, or pretend you didn't hear," as he once described it to a friend. All of that reminded Stan that however much he thought he belonged in the America of his day, however much he had become convinced that his Jewishness did not define him, the people around him had a different view.

All of this still remains relevant today. Albeit in ways less dramatic than for Stan, American Jews living in the twenty-first century still confront the issues that he wrestled with. To what extent are we defined by our American-ness, our Jewishness, or both? This question is particularly pointed in a country that is becoming more hostile to the outsider, more tribal, more anti-Semitic on the right, and more anti-Israel on the left. As we untangle issues of identity in America—are we American Jews, Jewish Americans, or just Americans?—there are other nagging questions that we cannot ignore and that bear fundamentally on how we see ourselves. What is our relationship to the State of Israel? And do we have obligations to our brothers and sisters there for whom the fight for a Jewish state continues, more than seventy years after Stan Andrews—artist, writer, and an assimilated and indifferent Jew—became one of the first fighter pilots in the history of the Israeli Air Force?

Authors' Note on the Use of "Palestine" and "Palestinian"

U ntil May 14, 1948, the area that today includes the State of Israel and the West Bank (the latter also referred to by some as Judea and Samaria) was collectively known as "Palestine." The Romans coined the name in 135 AD following the crushing of a Jewish revolt led by Bar Kokhba, as the Jews headed into what would be a nearly two-thousand-year exile from the land of Israel. There would not be an independent state of "Palestine" in the two millennia following the loss of Jewish independence, yet the name stuck.

It seems surprising now given the current political debate, but the word "Palestine" had an essentially Jewish connotation from the beginning of modern Zionism, right up until David Ben-Gurion's declaration of independence on May 14, 1948. In *The Jewish State*, Zionist visionary Theodor Herzl wrote: "Palestine is our ever-memorable historic home. The very name of Palestine would attract our people with a force of marvelous potency." At the First Zionist Conference in Basel,

Switzerland, in 1897, presided over by Herzl, the delegates passed a resolution announcing that "Zionism seeks to establish a home for the Jewish people in Palestine secured under public law." In his declaration of 1917, Britain's Lord Balfour stated: "His Majesty's Government view with favour the establishment in Palestine of a national home for the Jewish people...." The list goes on.

Therefore, consistent with the practice of the time, we use "Palestine" in describing the site of events in what is today Israel, that occurred during the period prior to May 14, 1948, and for events thereafter use "Israel." We use "Palestinian" to refer to occupants of Palestine, whether Jewish or Arab, during this same period, and "Israeli" for residents of the State of Israel after independence.

Chapter One

PRETTY BOY

You must remember that all my life I had heard of America—
everybody in our town had friends there or was going there
or got money orders from there. The earliest game I played
at was selling off my toy furniture and setting up in America.
All my life America was waiting, beckoning, shining—the
place where God would wipe away tears from off all faces.
—Israel Zangwill, *The Melting Pot* (1908)

I n the spring of 1909, young Joseph Anekstein left Lodz, Russia, for the long journey to America. He was a member of a mass Jewish exodus that, between 1881 and 1920, saw more than a million-and-a-half Russian Jews leave for new lives in the West.

The roots of this large-scale emigration lay in the government's systematic persecution of its Jewish citizens. The Jews of Russia were a people apart. Since soon after Russia's late eighteenth-century partition of Poland, an overwhelming majority were confined to an area that became known as the "Pale of Jewish Settlement." Jews were restricted in the professions they could pursue, the universities they could attend, and even their ability to teach the Russian language in their schools. These limitations trapped a substantial portion of the community in chronic poverty. At the end of the nineteenth century, some 40 percent of the Jews in the Pale were fully dependent on charity. Perhaps the most sinister policy subjected Jewish boys, sometimes as young as eight or nine, to a hellish, twenty-five-year period of military service. That service was often undertaken at remote military canton schools, where soldiers were sometimes forcibly converted to Christianity, assuming they were even able to survive the physical rigors of army life at such an early age.

Joseph had been a student at a higher-level Talmudic academy, open only to a particularly talented few. Among religious Jews like the Aneksteins, resistance to emigration was particularly high. They foresaw that life in America would be accompanied by a weakening of Jewish observance. They regarded the United States as a land where Jews would no longer keep the Sabbath, eat kosher food, or observe the many other rituals of religious life.

But Joseph was not to be dissuaded. He had more immediate concerns than the vagaries of future religious observance. Like many Jewish boys of his age—he was no more than seventeen when he left Russia—he feared being drafted into the czar's army. Further, after starting to work in a local garment shop, he had become part of an increasingly militant Jewish workers' movement. Strikes had led to crackdowns and arrests, and though Joseph had eluded imprisonment thus far, he realized that his luck could not hold much longer. It was time to get out.

Following the footsteps of many who had gone before him, Joseph crossed the Austro-Hungarian border illegally. From there he traveled by train to Germany, to the port city of Bremen. Like the typical immigrant of his day, he traveled without his parents whom he would not see again for years. In Bremen, Joseph found passage on the *Friedrich der Grosse* (Frederick the Great), a steamship that made the Atlantic crossing regularly. Joseph arrived at Ellis Island on May 5, 1909.

Before long, he had found employment in New York's thriving garment industry, contributing to the production of ladies' blouses, known as "shirtwaists." The shirtwaist business was thriving. Several years earlier, magazine illustrator Charles Dana Gibson had created the highly influential image of the Gibson Girl—a modern, sophisticated woman who favored shirtwaists and skirts. His creation sparked a fashion craze and with it an escalating demand for garment workers. By the beginning of the twentieth century, between one hundred fifty thousand and two hundred thousand Jews worked in the needle trades of New York.

Conditions in the factories were bitterly difficult. Wages were low and the workdays long. The factory floor was crowded and the employee-employer relationship was hostile. Workers were trailed to the bathroom and subjected to dignity-eroding searches before leaving the factory at day's end, lest they smuggle out a scrap of fabric. The term "sweatshop" was coined to describe the garment factories of Joseph's day— places where new immigrants were "sweated" to work longer and longer hours for less and less pay. Tuberculosis spread so easily among exhausted laborers in the cramped, poorly ventilated shops that it became known as the "Jewish" disease. The constant influx of young workers only made it easier for employers to resist calls for workplace reform.

The difficult conditions radicalized many of the new immigrants. Among Jewish workers, there was already a strong inclination toward pro-union and pro-socialist activity, particularly for those who, like Joseph, had been involved in the struggle for workers' rights in Russia. For many Jews, the labor movement became a substitute for the ideals of the Torah and the Talmud, the spiritual commitment to pursuing justice and bettering the world evolved into a desire to improve workers' lives.

Within a few years, Joseph met Rebecca Hoch, a fellow immigrant and garment worker. She had left Austria when her parents had tried to push her into an arranged marriage. Family lore held that there had been forty generations of rabbis in the Hoch family, but the chain of strict Jewish observance ended with Rebecca. She was fiery and free-spirited, an atheist, and a committed socialist. After a brief, intense courtship, she and Joseph were married.

Settling down in the Bronx, the two young immigrants had their first child, Esther, in 1912. A son was born two years later. For his name, Joseph took inspiration from Jewish philanthropist Isidor Straus who had perished with his wife during the sinking of the Titanic. He and Rebecca gave the boy the English name Irving and the Hebrew name Israel. In the family, Irving would always be "Is." For a decade, it seemed that this would be the entire Anekstein clan. But with Esther almost twelve and Is ten, another Anekstein child unexpectedly arrived. On April 23, 1923, Rebecca gave birth to a second son, Stanley.

To the older siblings, Stan was almost as much their child as he was Joseph's and Rebecca's. They looked out for him, doted on him, and helped him navigate the New World issues his parents did not understand. Despite the differences in age, the children grew remarkably close.

The family was captivated by Stan's striking looks from a very young age. Rebecca could not resist entering one favorite photo of her son in a beautiful child contest after he was already a teenager. The photo won, mortifying the adolescent Stan, particularly when his friends started calling him "pretty boy."

Life in the Anekstein household proceeded with almost no formal religious observance of any kind. The family didn't attend synagogue, even on the High Holidays. Neither Is nor Stan had a bar mitzvah. Yet, Joseph remained fervent in his Jewish identity. When Is and Esther decided to hang a stocking one Christmas for their little brother, their horrified father quickly tore it down. Socialist or not, there was a limit to the amount of assimilation he considered appropriate for the family.

A joyous spirit prevailed in the close-knit home. Joseph had a dry sense of humor, a love of poetry, and a strong singing voice. Rebecca, who continued to work, doted on her boys. At one point, she became convinced that Is wasn't growing fast enough, so she contacted a local healer who prescribed a treatment of fish oils. She later followed the same regimen with her younger son. Whether or not the result of this unconventional intervention, Stan's height shot up during his teenage years, setting him apart from his shorter classmates to such an extent that he felt awkward. By the time he was done growing, he was six feet tall.

Before Stan turned ten, Esther introduced him to art. Though a talented artist herself, she soon realized that her younger brother showed far more promise. Stan, always with a pencil in his hand, could draw any image that caught his fancy. As he moved from sketching to oil painting, it was clear to anyone who saw his work that he was destined for a career in art.

From his early school years, Stan was a presence. Even his walk made a statement of belonging. He was a precocious student, sometimes too much so for his dour teachers' liking. When Stan was in elementary school, an English teacher called his parents to complain about a classroom incident. The teacher explained that when she criticized something Stan had written, he had said, "If you take apart what an artist writes, you lose the quality of what an artist is trying to say." Esther, who had taken the call, commented that the statement was "quite remarkable," coming from such a young boy. Offended by the lack of deference, the teacher retorted that "the apple doesn't fall far from the tree" before hanging up in anger. Stan's bravado was no doubt a result of his strong academic success. He was skipped several times, finishing a junior high school program that included the ninth grade by the time he was thirteen.

Under New York's open enrollment policy, Joseph and Rebecca had the option of sending Stan to any public high school in the five boroughs. They chose DeWitt Clinton, near the family's apartment in the Bronx. The faculty there was outstanding; a tight Depression-era job market meant many of the teachers had PhDs. Unlike many of New York's public high schools, Clinton was single-sex. With nearly five thousand students, it was one of the largest all-boys secondary schools in the world.

The Clinton environment was a nurturing one for a Jewish boy from the Bronx. While its students came from all over the city, most were from the neighborhood, a mix of Jews, Irish, and Italians, with a smattering of intrepid blacks from across the river in Harlem. Almost without exception, these students were a responsible lot. They went to class, did their homework in the library, and stayed out of trouble.

Girls represented a special challenge to Stan early on, particularly given how young he was when he started at Clinton. Despite his good looks and outward confidence, he was awkward in his dealings with the opposite sex. It galled him that he was unable to initiate a conversation with one of the pretty Walton or Hunter girls that he would see on the subway. He often wondered if he would ever have his first sexual experience. It took a supreme effort to overcome his shyness, but he was determined. Eventually, Stan became a "sharpie"—a young man who dressed nicely, danced well, and had an easy conversational manner with the girls. Upon finding his voice, there was no turning back. Once, Rebecca came home to find Stan in the apartment with a girl. Unsure what to do, she immediately called Esther. "You have to do something about that boy!" she complained.

The high school years were ones of great academic accomplishment for Stan. Clinton's student body was talented and highly motivated. Clubs and committees catered to nearly every academic and avocational interest. Stan took full advantage of these opportunities. He was the art editor for three different student journals, a member of the school's art squad, and was on the publicity committee—the last of which created the posters for school dances, allowing Stan to tend to his two great passions: art and girls.

In the spring of 1939, he joined the art staff of the *Magpie*, the school's premier publication. The name had been inspired by a student in the 1920s, who described it as "a thing of shreds and tatters appropriate to magpies." Its intention was to be a serious literary offering, which, given the depth of talent at the school, was no pretense. One of Stan's co-contributors was Emile Capouya, whose literary career would include six years as editor of *The Nation*. Another, Richard Avedon, became one of the most renowned fashion and celebrity photographers of the twentieth century. Stan (Lieber) Lee, the legendary comic writer and creator of Spider-Man, X-Men, the Fantastic Four, Hulk, Iron Man, and Thor, was yet another member of the journal staff.[2] The students thrived on their intellectual camaraderie, spending hours together in the *Magpie*'s offices, discussing literature, politics, history, and religion.

Like his older brother before him, Stan was a brilliant student. The work came easily, and he found that he could get A's with little studying. While the typical Clinton student spent several hours a night on homework, Stan devoted a fraction of that time. But whatever he did was enough; after graduating, he earned membership in Arista, the school's honor society. Only 1 percent of the seniors achieved that distinction.

Stan's years at Clinton saw a great political evolution in the school and the United States as a whole. In the years after World War I, there was an increasing perception that American involvement had been a grave mistake, a view that 70 percent of Americans shared according to a 1935 Gallup poll. In 1934, a committee headed by Senator Gerald P. Nye of North

---

[2] In 1940, the year after Stan graduated, the *Magpie* contained the first published essay by James Baldwin, whose 1953 novel *Go Tell It on the Mountain* established him as a leading African American author of his generation.

Dakota charged that America had been tricked into war by munitions makers. The accusation further fueled isolationist sentiment. For most of the 1930s, Clinton boys were strongly anti-war in keeping with the national trend.

Outside Clinton's walls, though, the world was becoming a more dangerous place. Adolf Hitler became chancellor of Germany in January of 1933, and over the next two years, he consolidated his rule through the liquidation of political opponents and the dismantling of democratic institutions. In October 1935, Italy's Benito Mussolini sent his army into Ethiopia. A few months later, a civil war broke out in Spain, pitting Fascist troops under the command of General Francisco Franco, backed by Fascist Italy and Nazi Germany, against Royalist forces supported by the Soviet Union and the international Communist movement. The Japanese captured China's capital in 1937, unleashing a torrent of mayhem that became known as the Rape of Nanking.

By Stan's senior year, the rise of the Fascist powers and the fighting in Europe and Asia had begun to cause Americans to take notice of the dangers they could face, and student attitudes began to shift accordingly. The editor of the June 1939 *Magpie* wrote that "in Northern Europe, a madman is running amok and the world awaits his next move. And, in Southern Europe, and in the Far East, other less spectacular egomaniacs are mad for land and places in the Sun." It would not be long before the pacifists and isolationists of the 1930s were being shipped all over the world to do their part in the greatest military conflict in human history. Young Stanley Anekstein of the Bronx—artist, honor student, pretty boy, and sharpie—would be one of them.

Chapter Two

THE POOR MAN'S HARVARD

I changed mine. Did you?
—*Gentleman's Agreement* (1947)

n the summer of 1939, Stan graduated from Clinton. He had moved quickly through the ranks of New York's educational system and was only sixteen as he prepared for his next academic challenge. Like the majority of his classmates, he decided to remain in New York. He enrolled at City College, more popularly known by its initials CCNY.

CCNY had a special place in the hearts of first-generation Jewish-Americans like Stan, at a time when many of the country's finest educational institutions continued to openly discriminate against Jewish applicants. (As late as 1945, the president of Dartmouth College could still boast that a quota for Jewish enrollment permitted the school to focus on the "Christianization of its students.") City College was a place where the Cohens, Levys, and Bernsteins knew their religious backgrounds would not hold them back. Equally important, the school was free, a major benefit for working-class families. For the Aneksteins, as for approximately 80 percent of their fellow Americans at the time, the price of four years of study at a private university was simply out of reach.

CCNY, however, was hardly a school of last resort. It was one of the leading educational institutions of its day, producing eight Nobel laureates in the twentieth century, three who graduated while Stan was in high school and two who were students when he was there. One of Stan's friends was Leon Lederman, also of the class of 1943, who earned a Nobel Prize in Physics in 1988. CCNY fairly earned its nickname as the "Harvard of the Poor."

Before long, Stan's interests expanded beyond the world of art. Increasingly, he found himself attracted to writing. He had shown signs of promise at Clinton. A paper on the *Grapes of Wrath* had earned an A+, a feat that amazed his friends. In college, he worked to develop his talents further. When he looked to the future, he found that the dream of being an author was starting to crowd out his long-held vision of a life focused on art.

At Clinton, Stan became good friends with Gerry Finley, another boy from the neighborhood. The two spent so much time at each other's apartments that they knew the precise number of steps to get from one to the other. They developed a ritual; when it was time for the visitor to return home, the host would accompany him precisely one-half the number of steps between their apartments before heading back. The young men remained close while Stan was at CCNY, where Gerry also attended classes for a time. Stan sketched Finley, something Stan was turning into a regular gesture of friendship.

One day, late in 1942, Stan told Gerry that he was thinking of changing his last name. Stan did not explain why, and his friend, whose father had changed the family's name from Finkelstein to Finley, didn't ask for a reason. Gerry thought for a moment, then suggested "Andrews."

Some of Stan's motivation was practical. He thought that the name Anekstein was far too long and difficult to pronounce and he tired of correcting people. But the desire to change his last name also reflected Stan's discomfort with its obviously Jewish connotation. He was not embarrassed at being Jewish, but it bothered him that it was the first thing people thought when they heard his name. Many others at CCNY were doing the same thing—Sauls were becoming Pauls and Goldbergs were changing to Gilberts all around him—typically in response to pervasive discrimination against Jews in the workplace and elsewhere in American society. Famous Jews of the day were also Americanizing their names. Jacob Julius Garfinkle, another child of immigrant tailors, had become the actor John Garfield. Emanuel Goldenberg, whose immigrant family had arrived at Ellis Island only a few years before Joseph Anekstein, achieved fame as Edward G. Robinson.

In explaining the change to his family, Stan pointed to his upcoming military service. Instead of waiting to be drafted, he had decided to volunteer for the Army Air Corps. Stan wanted to become a fighter pilot and he worried that with a last name like Anekstein, he would be identified as a Jew and kept from pilot training. Joseph was upset with the decision and tried, in vain, to talk his son out of it. The name change would, in the end, have far-reaching consequences that neither father nor son could foresee.

Stan's dream of flying fighters was shared by a great many young men in the early 1940s. Fighter pilots had first captured the public's imagination during World War I, with riveting tales of dogfights in the skies over Europe involving the likes of American Eddie Rickenbacker, who recorded twenty-six kills during the conflict, and German ace Baron von Richthofen, the Red Baron. Dashing in his leather jacket, silk scarf, and goggles, the man at the controls of a fighter plane was the envy of all men and—at least it seemed to the aspiring flyers—the desire of all women. Popular culture reflected all this. "He Wears a Pair of Silver Wings" was one of the most popular songs of 1942, telling of a woman's love for her pilot beau: "Why, I'm so full of pride when we go walking/Every time he's home on leave/He with those wings on his tunic/And me with my heart on my sleeve." The idea that a pilot's wings could win over girls made all the sense in the world to Stan, who had spent many hours of his adolescence fantasizing about owning a car, which he was sure would guarantee him that elusive first sexual encounter.

With his last name now legally changed to Andrews, Stan signed up at the end of 1942 for the Enlisted Reserve Corps and was told to report in the spring of 1943. With the impending departure of so many members of its senior class, CCNY accelerated the semester. By March, not yet twenty years old, Stan had finished his coursework. Excelling once again, he was one of twenty-six members of the graduating class elected to the prestigious Phi Beta Kappa society.

Despite the shortened term, the seniors still managed to put together a yearbook. As he had done with so many student publications at Clinton, Stan volunteered for the art staff. He worked hard as part of a bright and talented group that made the most of their last creative endeavor before heading off to war. More than half a century later and having lost his vision, Marty Gold, one of Stan's collaborators, could still precisely describe the layout of the book from memory.

The extent of Stan's contributions befitted his informal title as "class artist." He prepared nine woodcuts, depicting the protectresses of the fine and liberal arts, to introduce the different sections of the book. He also helped illustrate one of the major themes—"Coming Events Cast Their Shadow"—with a pencil sketch of a soldier, sailor, and airman standing shoulder to shoulder, contrasted with a sketch of the same three in civilian clothes. There was no doubt where Stan saw himself in that tableau. The airman bears an unmistakable resemblance to the artist who drew him.

As he headed off to the army, Stan was leaving behind the only city he had ever really known. Gone would be the familiar neighborhoods, schools where he had achieved great success and social acceptance, and a circle of close and admiring friends. Though he did not fully realize it, his time in New York had been comfortable and protected. The life of a soldier would not only expose him to the physical dangers of wartime service but also, no less significant, to the loss of the protective social cocoon that had always been there for him.

Chapter Three

AN AIR FORCE MAN

The youth of America was under the spell of wings.
—Frederic Wakeman, *Shore Leave* (1944)

Stan's path to pilot's wings began with his strong suit: testing. At an army reception center, he completed a series of mental and physical examinations that were designed to determine whether a cadet was best suited to be a pilot, navigator, or bombardier. When the results were posted, Stan found his name on the coveted "Pilot" list.

Then the training began. In little more than two months, the army crammed students' heads with courses on the theory and practice of flight, physics, and Morse code, and tormented their bodies with long marches and other physical trials. All of it was meant to turn the men into officers and leaders, and standards were high. Guys were quickly washed out for poor performance or simply for having the wrong attitude.

Stan crossed the Mason-Dixon Line to continue his pilot training at an Army Air Forces base in Columbia, South Carolina. He started on a Stearman biplane, a single-engine aircraft he and the other cadets enjoyed flying. Still, the pressure to succeed was enormous. A cadet who failed to solo within eight hours washed out. That meant the loss of the chance at pilot's wings and an uncertain fate as a navigator, bombardier, or even back into the enlisted ranks as a gunner. Stan soloed and continued through the gauntlet. Next came the BT-13 "Vultee Vibrator" and then the AT-6. Each new plane meant more complexity and Stan and the other cadets didn't get comfortable until they had completed a few hours of flying. At each turn, with other cadets washing out all around them, the fear of failure was ever-present.

In more confident moments, Stan's thoughts turned to what lay ahead. Like most of the gung-ho recruits around him—all of whom had volunteered for pilot training—he was only vaguely concerned about the risk of dying. Instead, his anxiety was about how he would handle the stress of combat. He wondered whether fear would paralyze him at the critical moment when his crew's life hung in the balance, a concern he and the other would-be pilots knew to keep to themselves.

For much of their training, the cadets weren't told what kind of plane they would be flying in combat or, indeed, whether they would see action at all. Those like Stan who signed on to be fighter pilots continued to hold out hope that they would get their wish. To be sure, there was the appearance that cadets had a say in the matter, most pointedly when the army asked each man to write down his top three choices. But even listing "fighters, fighters, fighters," as one fellow cadet did, provided no guarantee that the eager recruit would get the chance to be the next Eddie Rickenbacker.

The American army of the 1940s was a rigid place. Men with flat feet were barred from the infantry, while those with glasses or color blindness had no hope of becoming pilots. When it was Stan's turn to get his assignment, the army decided that cadets weighing more than 150 pounds would go to bombers. If the fish oils from his childhood had helped him grow, they also succeeded in keeping the six-foot Stan, now above the maximum weight for fighter pilot training, out of the cockpit of a fighter.

While pursuing his pilot's wings, Stan sought out the charms of South Carolina's young ladies. Stan liked the local girls at first. Their lilting accents captivated him and he was relieved to discover that the same lines he had honed in New York retained their effectiveness down South. The Columbia girls danced with him and laughed at his jokes. They were also willing to go home with a handsome cadet they had met only hours earlier.

Stan soon realized, however, that there was an ugly side to the fun he was having. A lighthearted conversation with a pretty girl could suddenly turn nasty with a reference to "niggers." Any attempt to debate racial issues only poured gasoline on the fire. After a few attempts to defend the rights of Negroes, Stan simply retreated from these discussions, preferring not to hurt his chances at another conquest. But inside, he seethed.

Finally, after nearly twelve months of training and 229 flying hours, Stan was ready for the B-25 Mitchell bomber, the plane that he would ultimately fly in combat if he could remain on track. The B-25 was used primarily as a medium-altitude bomber, configured to drop its conventional payload on targets from seven thousand feet or higher. Control of the plane during a bombing run passed to the bombardier, who had a spectacular view of the target area from his Plexiglas enclosure below the cockpit. For defense against fighter attack, most Mitchells were fitted with two .50-caliber machine guns in the nose, two more in the top turret, two in the tail, and a fourth pair in the waist.

As Stan became increasingly comfortable in the left-hand seat of the B-25, he was nearing the end of the long and arduous process that would take a fine arts major from New York and turn him into the commander of a flying arsenal. Yet, as pleased as he was to still be on track to becoming a pilot, he could not completely shake the lost dream of flying fighters or "pursuits" as they were sometimes called. He was bored by the endless navigation flights, the tedious instrument training, and the dull bombing runs from more than a mile above the target. He was also frustrated by the lumbering performance of the B-25. On some training flights, Stan would catch a glimpse of a P-38 Lightning and yearn to be at its controls. He wanted to be alone in the sky, performing classic fighter-pilot maneuvers: rolls and snaps, loops and Immelmans. But for him such stunts were off-limits: "The B-25 is a bomber, not a pursuit plane," the pilot manual sternly reminded Stan and the other pilots who, of course, needed no such reminder.

Then again, not all aspects of bomber training were distasteful. Occasionally, the crews practiced bombing and strafing from extremely low altitudes—no more than fifty feet above the ground. As his plane streaked over the blurred landscape, guns blazing, Stan fully appreciated its speed and power. The best part was when the bombs were released and the B-25 briefly assumed the agile characteristics of a fighter, pulling over the target in a tight, twisting climb.

Stan finished the last phase of his stateside training in August. He and the other graduating cadets received their coveted wings as well as the bars of a second lieutenant. After nearly a year of training, it was time to go overseas. Stan received orders to report to California for deployment. He was off to war.

Chapter Four

TO THE PHILIPPINES

First we all go to the St. Mark and take a suite. Then we call for
room service. Then we drink. Then we go out and collect some
women. Then we take them to our rooms. Then we call room service.
That's as far as my plans go. After that, anything can happen.
—Frederic Wakeman, *Shore Leave* (1944)

Stan and a group of other flyers traveled to Sacramento, where they stayed for a month until their planes were ready for the trip overseas. Stan loved the place. It was a wide-open city, filled with servicemen on their way to war and attractive women eager to entertain them. It wasn't long before the guys were calling it "Shackramento." In the short time he was there, Stan virtually ran from woman to woman. At one point, he was living with one, meeting another at his hotel, and seeing a third on different nights. It was, he wrote to a friend, the "best town" he had ever been in.

With their interlude in California at an end, the men boarded their B-25s for Honolulu. The flight crews were lucky. They traveled by air rather than troopship, suffering only the discomfort of a long, cramped flight. To be sure, the flight to Hawaii was physically demanding. Stan flew for twelve hours and was so exhausted when he landed that he nearly collapsed when he got up to leave the cockpit.

Stan was disappointed to leave the pleasures of Sacramento, and he did not like Hawaii. He was uninterested in the islands' physical beauty, which he regarded as "garish," and he thought Honolulu a "dirty, narrow, crowded little town filled with unfriendly people." From his point of view, Coney Island had Waikiki Beach "beat by a mile." To Stan, the city's worst feature was its lack of eligible women. Many of the servicemen settled for the brothels, forming long lines that snaked along the sidewalks, like movie fans waiting to see the latest blockbuster. Stan would have none of that. He had a ladies' man's conceit and was appalled at the idea of paying for sex.

From Honolulu, the men continued west to Canton Island, a small, pork chop-shaped atoll halfway to Fiji. It was the next stop on the five-thousand-mile, hopscotch route that would take them on to Australia before ending on a base in the Southwest Pacific. But before he could leave Canton, Stan's march to war hit a detour. He had started feeling ill in Hawaii, but things got much worse in Canton, where a temperature of 105 degrees landed him in the hospital for an extended stay.

The source of the illness eluded diagnosis. Stan clearly had one of the innumerable tropical diseases that plagued servicemen in the Pacific, but the doctors had no idea which one. Nor could Sir Alexander Fleming, the inventor of penicillin who passed through on an inspection tour and who was asked to examine Stan, solve the medical mystery. Eventually, the fever subsided and, after nearly two months in the hospital, Stan had regained sufficient strength to continue his journey.

In December 1944, he finally arrived at the Far East Air Force—Combat Replacement and Training Center at Nadzab, New Guinea, for five weeks of training in Southwest Pacific warfare. New Guinea was in the portion of the theater under the command of Douglas MacArthur, the charismatic general who had been forced to flee the Philippines as the Japanese besieged his American and Filipino troops in the dark months following Pearl Harbor. MacArthur's air chief was George Kenney, a five-foot-six former MIT student who had been a fighter pilot during World War I. Kenney was interested in more effective ways to attack Japanese shipping lanes from the air. The immense distances in the Pacific required the enemy to transport and resupply troops by sea so air-to-ship attacks could cripple their war effort. But hitting a moving ship from a bomber cruising at five thousand feet had proven to be nearly impossible. Scoring a strike from altitude depended on too many variables—the rate of speed and direction of flight, the anticipated path of the falling bomb, and the speed and direction of the target itself.

Kenney theorized that low-altitude attacks would have more impact. He had at his disposal several squadrons of B-25 medium bombers, and he envisioned them streaking low over the water toward a Japanese ship then releasing a five-hundred-pound bomb with a delayed fuse. The bomb would skip across the waves like a flat stone on a pond until it slammed into the side of the target, then sinking for a few seconds before exploding below the water line, guaranteeing maximum damage.

The transformation of the B-25 into an anti-shipping weapon also called for a reconfiguration of its weaponry. While factory B-25s carried four pairs of .50-caliber guns, their purpose was as a defense against fighter attacks. Kenney had a more aggressive vision for them. Without sacrificing protection, he loaded the bomber with a bank of forward-firing machine guns that could be used in strafing attacks against shipping and ground targets alike. After some experimentation, he approved a jury-rigged design that replaced the bombardier's position in the nose with four guns and added a pair of "package" guns on each side of the plane's front.

Men like Stan who had received a traditional introduction to the B-25 now had to learn Kenney's low-altitude bombing and strafing tactics. Stan was entranced. He loved the feeling of speed as the plane skimmed low over the water, the roar and shake of the engines, the sensation of power as he opened up with the forward-firing machine guns, and even the smell of the acrid smoke that filled the pilot's compartment during an attack. After a few weeks, Stan was ready for combat.

As Stan completed his training, the Japanese were on the defensive throughout the Pacific. They faced a crippling one-two punch, with MacArthur advancing northward from New Guinea and Admiral Chester Nimitz's marine and naval forces cutting a bloody swath across the Central Pacific. MacArthur developed a "hit-'em-where-they-ain't" strategy that bypassed some of the strongest Japanese positions, cutting them off from their supplies and leaving them to rot on the vine, striking instead at less-defended areas that were closer to his ultimate objective. MacArthur then moved Kenney's air forces forward, deploying them with ever-increasing efficiency against the Japanese.

A critical exception to this strategy was MacArthur's determination to liberate the Philippines. Approaching from the direction of New Guinea in October 1944, MacArthur's forces landed at Leyte Gulf, nearly five hundred miles southeast of Luzon, the most populous of the Philippine islands. Just three hours after the first Allied troops landed, in one of the most famous scenes of World War II, MacArthur waded ashore to personally broadcast his return to Philippine soil.

By the new year, the time was right for an invasion of Luzon itself. On January 9, 1945, following a devastating naval bombardment, sixty-eight thousand men landed at Lingayen Gulf, north of Manila. Within five days, close to one hundred seventy-five thousand troops had gone ashore and secured a beachhead some twenty miles long. The Allies gained ground steadily and by early March had retaken Manila. While tens of thousands of Japanese troops remained dug in across the Philippine archipelago, the Allied forces controlled enough of the land to establish a number of local airfields on Luzon. MacArthur intended to use these to support further advances against the Japanese, and Kenney's modified B-25s were an essential component of that strategy. Luzon was where Stan was headed.

Chapter Five

AIR APACHE

Off we go into the wild blue yonder,
Climbing high into the sun;
Here they come zooming to meet our thunder,
At 'em boys, Give 'er the gun!
Down we dive, spouting our flame from under,
Off with one helluva roar!
We live in fame or go down in flame. Hey!
Nothing'll stop the Army Air Corps!
—"The Army Air Corps Song" (1939)

I n February, Stan received orders to report to the 345th Bombardment Group or the "Air Apaches." The name symbolized the type of lightning, ground-level warfare the B-25s practiced, which brought to mind the shock tactics of a raiding Indian war party from the Old West. The 345th was made up of four squadrons: the 498th, 499th, 500th, and 501st.

Stan was assigned to the 500th, the "Rough Raiders." Having sustained the highest losses in the group, the squadron had the greatest need for replacement crews.

The 345th was the first bomber group sent to the Philippines. By the time Stan reported, it had already moved forward to San Marcelino Airfield on Luzon, the most recent of five transfers the group had undertaken as part of MacArthur's leapfrog tactics. (The group continued to maintain some facilities at the old fields, leading one flyer to joke that "the sun never sets on the Apache Empire.") As the pace of success against the Japanese accelerated, so did the transfers. The current base, everyone knew, would be as temporary as the last. Once the area around Manila was secure, it would be on to Clark Field, the island's main airdrome.

Stan liked San Marcelino. The camp was laid out in a grassy valley, only a fifteen-minute walk from the airfield. Takeoffs could be a bit of a challenge—requiring a maneuver between two low mountain peaks—but the pilots all mastered it quickly. Stan lived with five other officers in a pyramidal tent with a dirt floor. Philippine villages and barrios surrounded San Marcelino and the men were soon interacting with the locals. Islanders were hired to do laundry, build bamboo chairs and tables, and run errands—often bartering their services for clothes. They were also regularly seen walking through the camp, hawking souvenirs, fresh fruits, and vegetables.

The Filipinos presented Stan with new sketching subjects. The girls were tiny and often older than they appeared; one who looked fourteen might really be in her early twenties and already the mother of several children. Although he found the locals to be excessively polite, Stan wasn't sure he trusted them. When they told him how much they loved the Americans and hated the Japanese, he couldn't help but wonder if they had said the opposite to their previous occupiers.

With the rainy season over, the days at San Marcelino were oppressively hot. Those who weren't flying spent the afternoons reading or writing letters in their bunks or shooting the breeze with their tentmates. Sometimes, Stan grabbed a piece of army stationery and did a quick pencil sketch of a friend. They played sports, mostly volleyball or horseshoes, and watched movies almost every night, projected from the back of an ambulance. Still, there was no mistaking that this was the army. The washing facilities (usually a helmet) and latrines (holes in the ground) were the subjects of vigorous griping, as was the food, which Stan rated as "piss poor."

Stan found the other members of the squadron friendly but reserved. The men of the 500th had learned to insulate themselves against some of the emotional cost of losing fellow flyers in combat. There was an unwritten rule that the veterans did not form friendships with men who had flown less than five missions with the squadron. Those first missions were considered the most dangerous since the new flyers were still learning. There was nothing harder than losing a friend in war.

As a newly arrived pilot, Stan was not given immediate command of an aircraft. Protocol required replacement pilots to fly those critical first five missions as copilots so they could watch and learn how the Rough Raiders worked. In the early evening of March 4, a sheet of paper on the squadron bulletin board announced a mission scheduled for the next morning. It began as they always did with "To: All Concerned," before listing the members of the crews who would be taking part. Stan's name was on the list. According to the announcement, the men needed to be up at 5 a.m., prepared for roll call at 5:50, at the aircraft line at 6:00, and in their planes by 6:30. Takeoff was at 7:00.

The group intelligence officer briefed the crews that night, after the movie. He explained that the men would be participating in an anti-shipping strike off the coast of Indo-China (today Vietnam), looking for targets between Phan Rang Bay and Tourane (today Da Nang). The flyers would be in the air a long time; just getting to the target would take more than four hours. They would arrive around midday when visibility and weather conditions were the best. Assuming the mission went smoothly, the fighting would be over in less than thirty minutes. Then they would fly the four hours back to base and a well-earned rest.

On the morning of March 5, the six B-25s roared out of San Marcelino, right on schedule. For most of the route, they flew at three thousand five hundred feet, scanning for targets. Planes from another squadron spotted Japanese vessels near Cape Hapoix and attacked. When their ammunition was expended, they called in the six Mitchells from the 500th to continue the assault. Shortly after 11 a.m., Stan's plane drew within range and dropped to eight hundred feet. Over the course of forty minutes, the crew noticed four sub chasers, a small transport craft known as a "lugger," two coastal freighters, and a flotilla of more than one hundred junks.

Preparing for the attack, the six planes dropped below one hundred feet and pulled into a line-abreast formation to maximize the coverage of their machine guns while limiting the risk of friendly fire. Stan's plane swooped down on one of the freighters, machine guns fully opened up, and skipped a five-hundred-pound bomb at the target. They picked out a second freighter and made a couple of attack runs over it—seeing bomb splashes around the vessel, followed by the spray of an explosion. Anti-aircraft fire from one of the ships in the harbor added to the chaos. Avoiding the enemy fire, Stan's B-25 roared out of the harbor so quickly he didn't see what happened, but the crew of another aircraft confirmed the sinking of the second freighter. It was a dazzling introduction to aerial warfare, Apache-style, and Stan was thrilled.

On March 10, in his third mission in less than a week, Stan took off in one of six B-25s continuing the pursuit of the Japanese shipping routes off the coast of Indo-China. As the planes came within range of Tourane Bay, Stan's line of vision was filled with the most impressive array of targets he had yet encountered: two tankers—one a ten-thousand-tonner, the second a quarter the size—and four smaller vessels. Stan's plane, piloted by Robert Van Scoyk, made for the big ship. Streaking over the bay at mast height, it strafed the entire length of the tanker's deck, evading the barrage of anti-aircraft fire from the desperate Japanese gunners, some of whom could be seen dropping from the .50-caliber shells. Van Scoyk then skipped two five-hundred-pound bombs toward the tanker's side. They struck near the stern, and the flyers watched as a cloud of smoke rose from the vessel. Subsequent aerial reconnaissance confirmed the sinking of the tanker.

The intelligence officer who debriefed the participants in the raid singled out Van Scoyk's plane in his report of that day's performance, recommending that each member of his crew receive an Air Medal. The higher-ups agreed. General Kenney personally signed a letter to Stan's parents, notifying them of the award. Stan was delighted. Herb Linden, a good friend from New York, had already won a Distinguished Flying Cross for supply flights over the hump in the China-Burma-India Theater, and Stan was looking to keep pace. That would not be easy because medals were seen as especially hard to come by in the Southwest Pacific, as compared to other theaters. He heard that guys flying in Europe were receiving Air Medals for every five missions and a Distinguished Flying Cross for every twenty-five, regardless of results. Stan and the others in the Southwest Pacific liked to joke about the China-Burma-India pilot who got a Purple Heart because he cut his finger flipping on the automatic pilot.

After Tourane Bay, Stan needed just two more missions to fill out his quota of flights in the copilot seat, one off the coast of China and another over Hong Kong. With that, Stan's apprenticeship was over. He was ready to command his own B-25. As a first pilot, Stan began to engage the veterans, feeling more a part of the squadron. As he got to know them all better, he noted with amusement the existence of two cliques among the flyers: the "old combat men," who were convinced that conditions had been much tougher when they first arrived, and the "new boys," like Stan, to whom the old guard mostly condescended. "You shoulda been here when it was tough" was a familiar refrain that usually preceded a lengthy description of harsh times at a prior base or more intense missions from the past. The fresh pilots soon learned the appropriate retort: "Give us a few thousand words on how hot you are."

As he became more comfortable as a member of the squadron, Stan internalized its slang. A "jock juggler," a phrase that one plane carried on its nose, was a mission in which the aircraft was likely to be lost. "Hanging your jock" meant being shot down or killed. That one particularly resonated with Stan, capturing what he regarded as an appropriately nonchalant, even contemptuous, view of death. A "wheel" was a big shot, who lived, appropriately enough, in a "wheel house." Though Stan had been pleased to become an officer and aspired to higher rank, he instinctively distrusted "wheels" and it was a label that he applied derisively. His respect was reserved for the men who flew the missions. Finally, there were the curses, a necessity for any wartime unit. Tough shit was "hardships," and "booger" or "bugger" meant fuck, as in "booger up" or "booger you" or "bugger off."

Before March ended, Stan had completed two missions as a first pilot. The pace of his flying—seven missions in twenty days—was indicative of the strain on the squadron as a whole. The Rough Raiders had lost a little over a quarter of their planes and personnel in a month. Anyone in flying condition could expect to see his name posted on the bulletin board multiple times each week.

Two days after participating in a twenty-six-plane raid on Lamsepo, Stan was in the sky again, off Hainan. In less than a week, he had flown over Formosa, Luzon, and China. Like servicemen in other parts of the world, Stan and the other flyers collected paper currency from the different countries they had been in—or over—during the war. They taped them together end to end creating a chain called a "short snorter." At the officer's club, crewmen pulled theirs out to compare and the flyer with the shortest one had to buy the drinks.

Acutely aware that for most of his life he had barely ventured beyond the crowded confines of New York City, Stan felt changed by the places he had seen. He joked about it in a letter to his friend Herb Linden: "All in all I'm developing a well-rounded personality. They always say that travel broadens one, and it does, if you live through it."

Chapter Six

PRAYER MEETINGS AND NEW TARGETS

An American soldier in Europe, even though the towns may be 'off limits' to him or destroyed completely, still has a sense of being near civilization that is like his own. But out here there is nothing like that. You are on an island, the natives are strange people, there's no city and no place to go. If you had a three-day pass, you'd probably spend it lying on your cot. Eventually, boredom and the 'island complex' starts to take hold.
—Ernie Pyle (1945)[3]

Amid the grueling schedule of missions, the guys did find time to unwind. Sometimes they took a jeep to the nearby naval base at Subic Bay, where the Apaches could use the

---

[3]   Quoted in *Ernie's War: The Best of Ernie Pyle's World War II Dispatches* (David Nichols, Ed.) (1986).

navy clubs. Twenty-five-cent highballs were a squadron favorite. But when the men received passes for off-base R&R (rest and recuperation), the chosen destination was Manila. By jeep, it could be a four- or five-hour slog over mountains through the aptly named Zig-Zag Pass. Occasionally, they got to make the trip by air. Naval officers occasionally tagged along for the ride, and the pilots couldn't resist having fun at the expense of men with little flying experience. They roller-coastered their B-25s across Manila harbor, dropping down on the deck, pulling up briefly to barely clear one of the wrecks that still littered the bay after the battles from months earlier, and then diving for the water again. The maneuvers invariably made the navy men sick, to the delight of the flyers.

But the Rough Raiders didn't need to leave San Marcelino to cut loose. Early on, Stan was initiated into the squadron's "prayer meetings." They were called whenever a crew member was lost, when someone received a "Dear John" letter, or for any other excuse that someone could come up with. Lugging their own chairs and canteen cups, the guys crammed into one of the tents to drink, sing, and swap stories—once squeezing forty-eight men into a tent for a particularly memorable "meeting." Finding something to drink was a bit of a challenge since liquor was hard to come by. The solution was often solved with Filipino whiskey, made from fermented palm sap, which the men topped off with a mixture of lemon powder, sugar, and chemically treated water from rubber bags that everyone hung in their tents. Before pouring the concoction into their aluminum cups, the flight surgeon tested it just to make sure it wouldn't blind anyone. It was powerful stuff; the Raiders joked that it gave you a hangover so strong you had to bang your head against the flagpole the next morning to move the pain to the outside.

Over a three-day period from the 10th of May to the 12th, the group moved from San Marcelino to Clark Field. For the Rough Raiders, it was a welcome change. While San Marcelino had been better than some of the earlier Pacific bases, Clark was almost like being on a base back home. There was running water, wood to build shacks or at least cover the dirt floor of a pyramidal tent with, cheap liquor, and much better food than the men had eaten since heading out to the Pacific. A nearby army base even had tennis courts and swimming pools. Of particular interest to Stan and the others was the presence of so many women—nurses, Red Cross workers, and members of the Women's Army Corps (WACs)—who flocked to the officers and enlisted men's clubs that were opening all over the complex. As if the improved conditions at the base were not enough, the group claimed two houses in Manila for R&R: one for enlisted men and one for the officers. There, the men experienced the excitement of a bustling wartime city with its bars, prostitutes, and other diversions.

The war pressed on, leaving little time to savor the new surroundings. On May 13, the day after the move to Clark was complete, Stan was back in the air on a mission against the remnants of Japanese forces still dug in on Luzon. On that flight, he damaged a wing when he dropped too low, striking some branches. A week later, his plane took a bullet in the right wing during a second Luzon strike. In three of four missions that May, Stan's plane suffered damage and he was developing a reputation as an aggressive pilot.

For the first two weeks of June, the squadron focused on training as weather conditions worsened over Formosa. The squadron received several B-25s fitted with rockets and the crews needed to learn how to use the new weapon. The break from combat operations also gave the men an opportunity to sharpen their skip-bombing skills, and they made repeated attack runs on a wreck lying off the coast near San Marcelino. Even training flights could be dangerous, however. In April, Stan crash-landed following one of these. A few months later, he was given a new B-25 to take up for a short flight in order to break in the engines and ready the plane for combat. One of the engines caught fire and Stan had to set the plane down immediately. He landed safely, but the Mitchell was a total loss. He laughed off his two brushes with disaster, joking about having a propensity for crashing. Behind the jokes, he was unmistakably proud that he had managed to walk away unscathed, reinforcing an emerging sense that he would always survive.

Stan loved the Air Apache style of combat. It was, as he characterized it to Herb Linden, "really my meat." He liked being able to watch his tracers run their deadly tracks up and into a machine gun pit and see the enemy fire come to a stop. Whether it was a ship, a train, or a building, he could pick out a target, go right after it, and know immediately if he had succeeded. It made the war immediate and close and helped Stan feel like he was part of something significant. If he couldn't be in the cockpit of a fighter, this was at least a close second.

Stan, though, was not completely oblivious to the dangers he faced. His nerves sometimes got the better of him during the preflight briefing. Suddenly, the equipment would seem to hang heavily on his body and even the contents of his pockets bothered his skin. His stomach would tighten, leaving him with no appetite. On these few occasions, the nervousness only increased during the mission. It felt like the fear was both inside and outside of his body—squeezing his stomach and chest, drying his lips, and forming beads of sweat on his neck. Like many of the men, he resorted to a number of tricks to try to keep the fear at bay. He joined in pre-mission bets over coveted .45s, Aussie boots, or flight jackets, with the loser being the one who failed to return. The wagers seemed cruel and insensitive to the squadron's new arrivals but useful to Stan and the other old-timers in maintaining their nerve.

In July, it was again time for the squadron to move and soldiers began dismantling administration buildings and loading the equipment into crates. The flight crews moved out first, taking their B-25s over to Ie Shima (now Iejima), a tiny, ten-square-mile island off the coast of Okinawa and only three hundred fifty miles from the southern coast of Honshu. It was, in July of 1945, the closest Allied air base to the Japanese home islands.

The primary mission on Ie Shima was to blockade Japan's southern islands. Despite mines in the harbors and roving American submarines, small enemy ships continued to ply the waters between Korea and Japan, bringing food to the starving population. The Air Apaches were ordered to put an end to this traffic, further tightening the noose around Japan.

By the time the base moved and refresher training was completed, it was nearly August. On the 6th, Stan flew his first raid over Korea seeking out Japanese ships near the port city of Pusan (now called Busan). He was part of a four-plane element that sank a gunboat and two small freighters. One of the B-25s took a direct hit, plunging into the water, and exploding on impact. Despite all the losses they were suffering, the Japanese could still put up a strong fight. The move to Ie Shima put the Air Apaches in range of some of the strongest air defenses they had seen since early in the war. Between July 29 and August 9, the group lost ten crews and nearly a full squadron's worth of planes.

Although the men of the 500th did not learn of it until the next day, August 6 saw the most dramatic development in the Pacific War since the attack on Pearl Harbor. That morning, a lone B-29 dropped the first atomic bomb on Hiroshima, wiping out the city. The men became consumed with speculation about whether the Japanese would continue the war after the destruction. For many in the squadron, this ushered in the most stressful part of their wartime service. While an end to the fighting seemed to be within reach, operations continued and Ie Shima itself came under Japanese air attack several times. To the men, it seemed that this would be an especially unfortunate time to be hit.

On August 8 and 9, Stan again took part in raids off the Korean coast. Of thirty-one planes that participated in the first of them, nine suffered damage and one was forced to ditch. These missions again coincided with seismic events in the Pacific War. On August 8, the Russians declared war against the Japanese, sending 1.6 million men into Manchuria. The next day, the Allies dropped the second atomic bomb, this time over Nagasaki.

The August 9 mission, which again brought Stan near the Korean port of Pusan, was his 44th of the war. It was also his last. The next day, the Japanese announced that they were prepared to surrender and the Pacific fighting was suddenly over. An Air Apache raid was in the air that day, but a message from headquarters caught the B-25s before they reached the target, giving the relieved flyers the news and calling them back to base.

The men convened one last prayer meeting to celebrate the fighting's end, the first big gathering since San Marcelino. They sang all the old classics, but the mood was different, with the soldiers already emerging from the unremitting strain of combat and looking toward the future. Stan, though, was one of the few Rough Raiders who was in no hurry to get out of the army. Months earlier, he had decided that he would remain in the air corps even after he had earned sufficient points to return home, hoping to make captain. As much as he resented the wheels or, more specifically, the "paddlefeet" who did not fly combat, he was keen on the idea of achieving rank. Like medals or school grades, rank was, to him, a clear barometer of success.

In the days immediately following the war's end, Stan kept himself busy. On August 13, he sketched one squadron buddy and a few days later he flew one final time. With the announcement of Japan's surrender, reporters from all over the Pacific rushed to the area, hoping to catch a flight to see the home islands. The destinations on everyone's minds, of course, were the two atomic bomb sites, and Ie Shima was a perfect jumping-off point. Several B-25s, including one piloted by Stan, were assigned to take journalists over Nagasaki on a low-altitude tour of the destruction.

The planes headed north until the pilots saw a dark spot on the horizon. Stan picked out Nagasaki lying atop a hill near a bay. They passed the bay's entrance, cleared a ridge, and swung east, dropping to one thousand feet. As they drew closer, they descended to what would have been tree-top height. Stan saw fewer than a half-dozen buildings, each leaning precariously with their insides exposed. He also noticed some trolley tracks, which had miraculously emerged from the explosion untwisted. Most striking, though, was the red dust that covered everything, as if a deranged giant had repeatedly beaten the whole city with a rusty pipe.

Stan finished his first pass, pulled up and into a wide circle, and came around for a second run over the ruined city. He saw a few survivors, some dragging carts and wagons loaded with bundles. Several looked up and waved at the planes. Stan also saw a white stone chimney, lying intact amid the ruins of a very large building, and several bodies lying on the ground. With two passes, they had seen all there was to see and turned for the trip back to Ie Shima.

As the days and weeks passed, there was a great deal of uncertainty about where the Air Apaches would go next. There were all sorts of rumors. Some said the group would be disbanded, while others heard it would be moved to Korea. Eventually, the men learned they would be going home, but no one was sure when. September came, then October and November, and still, the Apaches lingered at Ie Shima, waiting for a troopship that would finally release them from their limbo. Stan described the frustration that he and the others felt in a letter to his sister Esther: "We wake up every morning and think 'Well, maybe, this is the day the boat's coming in.' And we go to sleep each night and say—'Well, maybe, it'll be here when I wake up in the morning.' But it never is."

At the same time, Stan recognized the ludicrous humor of their situation: "If you want a sure way to drive men collectively neurotic, this is it. Put them on a rock in the middle of the ocean, 3 miles wide by 5 miles long. Sprinkle it with a few trees and lots of coral. Make it dry + dusty when the suns out, + muddy and cold when it rains. Throw in a 155-mph typhoon every month or so to blow the tents away, so they can put them up again in time for the next one. Make the food a constant diet of powdered eggs, dehydrated potatoes, bully beef, spam, + hash—no milk, fresh eggs, fresh meat, fresh vegetables, but about once every three months or more, give them one good meal, say on Thanksgiving, so they can remember what good food is like, and miss it more. Make the bulk of the amusements on the island an occasional movie, shown from a bad movie projector on a torn screen, with a faulty soundtrack, and in the rain. Throw in a few books now and then, chiefly Westerns, so they'll remember how to read.

"But, most important, keep them in suspense. First rush them like mad to get processed, all papers in order, bags set to go—and then let them wait. Tell them a boat will come in any day—you don't know when but you'll be sure to let them know. But don't set a definite date. Give them field glasses so they can climb a hill and search the empty horizon for ships, any ship, but never any in sight. Tell them they'll be home by Thanksgiving, then maybe Christmas, or perhaps New Years. Let the days stretch into weeks, and the weeks into months. But keep them waiting, keep them waiting. There's nothing like waiting for a good disposition."

Though the wait was maddening, a familiar project kept Stan busy. The base assembled a staff of artists and writers to create a memory book. To Stan, it was going to be another yearbook project like the one at CCNY, and he happily signed on to help.

The completed volume, *Warpath*, traced the Air Apaches from activation in November 1942, their advance across the Southwest Pacific over the next two years, and the final months of combat. Each of the four squadrons was the subject of a section. Stan created the opening panel for the Rough Raider chapter, featuring the squadron logo above a pilot wearing a leather jacket. In the panel, the pilot holds his hands in front of him, at an angle and turned sideways, in the classic pose of an airman describing a just-completed mission. Like the pilot in the CCNY yearbook, this one also bears a strong resemblance to the artist who sketched him.

Stan also contributed several essays to *Warpath*. In "Prayer Meeting," he described the beloved ritual: "In these gatherings, religion was not the main theme. To put it bluntly, the main idea at a Prayer Meeting was to get good and drunk—and have a lot of fun doing it. For it was around the songs that most Prayer Meetings revolved. Much can be said about our Squadron songs, very little of it printable.... You could do a great deal of introspective delving to find the psychological reason for these songs. Let's put it simply and call them a release. There isn't much to do in the Pacific, and chastity is enforced by geography. This was our chance to be wicked and there was no one to be shocked."

In a closing piece, he pondered what the war would continue to mean to the Rough Raiders: "Perhaps, then, we can look in somewhat calmer retrospect, over a period of our lives, easily distinct from all others in our experience. Distinct and distinguishing, for combat men are marked indelibly, not always similarly, but always definitely. It may be in a studied arrogance, or in amused tolerance of the ground men. It may be in a marked disrespect for the mores and morals of conventional *hoi polloi*. Or it may be in the nervous twitch, the involuntary shudder, the recurrent nightmares of those who have been too close to Death for too long a time."

Stan went on to muse about death, which "was always there, riding with us." It was, he asserted, "the ultimate purpose in conflict, the driving force of the combat man." Yet, "too long association with its influence has had its effects." He concluded by wondering if the men of the squadron would be "forever apart in mind and heart from those who have not experienced what we have." For Stan, the question was particularly apt.

Chapter Seven

CALIFORNIA

Oh I'm packing my grip
And I'm leaving today
Cause I'm taking a trip California way
—"San Fernando Valley," Bing Crosby (1944)

I n the last days of 1945, Stan finally set foot again in New York. As he announced to Herb Linden, "the prodigal has returned." With nearly two months of terminal leave to kill before he was formally out of the service, he was not a civilian yet. He didn't mind the extra time in uniform, though. With his pilot's wings and newly-earned captain's bars, he cut a dashing figure in the eyes of the local women.

First, though, there were reunions with the family. Stan went to see his sister Esther, driving a 1942 Nash that he had wasted no time picking up. He was excited to see her two young daughters, who had been too small to remember him when he went off to war. As his older sister waited on the curb with her heart in her throat, he took the girls on a wild car trip through the neighborhood, whipping around corners and causing them to slide all over the back seat. It was a roller coaster ride they never forgot, sharing the memory with Jeff more than sixty years later. When Stan wasn't careening around a corner, he talked with them about their interests. Much of the conversation was about art, for which Stan's older niece had a real talent. Back at Esther's building, a group of WACs and WAVES who lived in the neighborhood walked by. When they saw Stan, a captain, they saluted, and the nieces loved it. They stood outside and saluted him also, mimicking their uncle's more mature female admirers.

Within a week of his return, the contours of Stan's future plans began to take shape. He would loaf for a week or two, then take art classes for six months to refresh his skills. After that, he would pursue a master's degree in art on the GI Bill. But he was finished with CCNY. For his postwar studies, he had his sights set on Los Angeles and UCLA in particular.

Stan was hardly unique among returning veterans in looking to create a new life on the West Coast. Millions of servicemen had spent time there for training or, like Stan, on the way to the Pacific theater, and that taste of sunshine and open space had hooked them. More than eight hundred thousand would move to the Golden State in the years right after the war. Bing Crosby captured the sentiment in his 1944 hit "San Fernando Valley": "I'm gonna settle down and never more roam; and make the San Fernando Valley my home."

Like other returning veterans who were anxious to make up for time lost during the war, Stan was already starting to take a long-term view of what his future in the West would look like. With the master's degree, he would also get a teaching credential. That would allow him to teach art, while still tending to his own aspirations as an artist through freelance projects in his spare time.

Not every aspect of Stan's planning was focused on the practical aspects of career building, however. The 1940s were the golden age of movies, and Stan was not immune to the lure of Hollywood. In the back of his mind, he harbored dreams of landing a high-paying creative job with a major movie studio. Choosing a school in LA also nourished the lighter side of Stan's postwar planning.

There was still a lot of time until the next school term started in the fall of 1946 and Stan was determined to remain productive. Before January was over, he had enrolled in several classes at the Pratt Institute in Manhattan, looking to sharpen art skills that had not been challenged by much more than the occasional twenty-minute pencil sketch during the war. He enjoyed Pratt from the start. Clinton had been an all-boys school and CCNY was virtually single-sex as well. Pratt, on the other hand, was fully coed. Still resplendent in his pilot's uniform, Stan loved it. As he wrote to Linden: "You know, this is the first co-ed school I've ever attended, and I really think they have something." One of his dates was Miss Red Cross of 1946, another was a Conover model. It was a remarkable change of scenery for someone who, until recently, had been stuck on a Pacific atoll with virtually no female companionship of any kind.

It was not all fun and games, however. Pratt was a serious art school, and there were regular assignments. Stan immediately felt the impact of the years away from the formal study of art. As he complained to Linden: "3 years of advanced laying around in the Air Corps is not the best preparation for work."

Looking toward the summer, Stan was tempted to try to find a job at Grossinger's in the Catskills, a resort that catered to an overwhelmingly Jewish clientele from the city, where he had worked over vacations while in high school. He thought he might want to get back his old job as a waiter, while spending his evenings engaged in romantic pursuits, and asked Herb Linden to go with him. Now that Stan was a pilot, he also thought it might be possible to find work ferrying wealthy patrons from New York up to the resort.

The idea of going back to waiting tables, though, soon lost its appeal, and any thoughts about spending the summer as a pilot were scrapped, once he learned that there were no nearby airfields to accommodate a charter service. The resort manager was intrigued by the idea of landing planes on the lake, but Stan did not have access to an amphibious plane or, for that matter, know how to land one. He now began to focus entirely on the move to Los Angeles.

Stan hoped to persuade Herb Linden and Gerry Finley to join him on the journey. He talked to them not just about starting fresh in California but also about the good times they would have on the way there. He had put down a deposit on a Buick convertible and hoped to have the car in time for the trip. They could take it slow on the cross-country drive, seeing sights, stopping in towns that caught their fancy, and looking up girls he had known during his time in the service. The picture he painted convinced Finley. Linden, though, had just taken a job in New Jersey and was not ready to alter his plans so dramatically.

In March, Stan's fantasy about landing a job in the movie industry suddenly seemed within reach. Esther's husband Sam, through a friend of his boss, had a contact with Hollywood titan Albert Warner. Sam believed that, working through his contact, he might be able to get Stan his start as a movie artist. Stan was thrilled and at the same time amused at the whole thing. As he explained it in a letter to Linden:

"[A] few days ago…my brother-in-law had a talk with his boss (or rather senior partner). Said boss is a very close friend of Major Albert Warner of a small firm called Warner Bros. of which you may have heard in connection with Errol Flynn on Pg. 4 of the New York Daily News. Said boss also loves my brother-in-law like a brother. My name, aspirations, and talents (too numerous to mention, of course) just happened to crop up in the conversation, plus the fact that I was recently a very hot captain, shedding blood for his country and said b. solemnly assured my b. in l. that he could get me an art job in the Warner Bros. studio anytime, like *that* (*that* is to be illustrated by an appropriate snapping of the fingers). This seems to be straight poop, since my b. in l. (whom we shall hereinafter refer to as "Sam") is ordinarily a very skeptical and cautious individual, and doesn't usually get as enthusiastic over things like this."

Stan now began to envision a glamorous one-hundred-dollar-a-week job, doing, he imagined, almost nothing at all. Yet, he tried to remain realistic. As he summed it up to Linden: "So, that's the way it stands—I *am* going to Hollywood. If I get a job in Warner Bros.—well and good. If not, I'll go to school for a year, and then look for a job. But I am going—and this summer, too."

By June, it was clear that the Buick was not going to be delivered in time, its yearning owner-to-be just one more victim of the postwar car shortage. So, Stan and Finley loaded up the Nash and headed west. But now that they were actually on the road, the pair was more focused on the trip itself rather than the stops along the way. Neither had much driving experience—Stan had spent far more time at the controls of an airplane than behind the wheel of a car—and both were intent on logging as much time as possible in the driver's seat. They settled on trading control of the wheel every one hundred miles. Whoever was in the passenger seat watched the odometer intently, urging the driver to pull over at the precise moment the digits rolled over, regardless of where they happened to be.

As they traversed the Rockies, during one of Finley's turns at the wheel, the Nash hit a patch of ice, an uncharted hazard for the novice driver. The car skidded off the road and flipped into a ditch, resting on its roof. Battery acid leaked from the engine compartment onto the windshield, destroying it. Neither of the men was hurt, though, and the car was still drivable.

With help, they got the car righted and rolling again, but something needed to be done about the windshield. They visited a local junkyard and found a used one that almost fit. With no choice, they took the replacement. For the remainder of the drive to California, the nondriver had to sit with his feet directly on the windshield, pressing it up against the window frame and preventing it from falling back into the car. After a few days of awkward driving, they were in Los Angeles.

Postwar LA had the feel of an Old West boomtown. The population was exploding. Local bars and clubs were a magnet for colorful gangsters, restless former soldiers, and pretty women lured by the glamour of Hollywood. A contemporary writer described the city as one big cocktail lounge with every stool occupied by a female available for pick-up. The Los Angeles of 1946 was, it seemed, the perfect place for Stan.

Chapter Eight

TO ALL CONCERNED

There are no atheists in foxholes.
—Unknown Author (1942)

UCLA in the fall of 1946, like so many colleges and universities across the country, was experiencing a wave of enrollment courtesy of the GI Bill. That term the school had 14,151 students, a new record. Of those, more than 40 percent were veterans, and they were a dominant presence. The school's largest social organization was Cal-Vets, which arranged dances, sports events, picnics, parties, and local trips in an effort to make student life more enjoyable for the university's returning soldiers.

Nestled on a hill overlooking the LA suburb of Westwood, its buildings surrounding a lush Romanesque quadrangle, UCLA represented a dramatic change of scenery for a New

York boy who had previously only experienced urban campuses. Politically, though, it suited Stan. It was liberal, racially mixed (Jackie Robinson was a graduate), and religiously diverse with many Jewish students. Indeed, the UCLA of that time was sometimes described as the "CCNY of the West."

As the school year began, Stan was settling nicely into his new life in LA. His circle of friends expanded to include Harold Lachs, the brother-in-law of Stan's older brother Is. Lachs was also a veteran of the Pacific War as well as an artist, and he and Stan took a sculpture class together. However, while Stan was continuing to refresh and improve his artistic skills, he was also eager to attend to his other great ambition—becoming a writer.

At various times during his service in the Pacific, Stan had tried his hand at writing. His first efforts, in longhand, were short stories that explored the feelings of an air corps man in the process of becoming a bomber pilot; the impotence of flying as copilot; the thrill of low-altitude attack runs; an unrequited desire to fly fighters; and the difficulty of relating to crew members who came from markedly different, typically southern, backgrounds. While ostensibly fictional, many of the stories closely tracked Stan's actual experiences and mirrored his attitudes. Those on flying were particularly reflective of the real Stan with his protagonists parroting the same kinds of things that he had told Herb Linden or other close friends countless times.

After he enrolled in an English composition class, Stan's output immediately increased. Still using soldiers as main characters, he now took on larger themes. He found himself coming back again and again to the meaning of the World

War II expression: "There are no atheists in foxholes." Stan, who regarded himself as an agnostic, often wondered whether someone who didn't believe in God would be moved to pray when confronted with imminent death on the battlefield.

Stan's other favorite subject, to which he devoted an enormous amount of creative energy, was anti-Semitism. Stan's essays in the Air Apache memory book *Warpath* had reflected what he believed to have been the general experience of the typical flyer in the unit. Those things mattered to Stan as well and he had liked his time with the squadron. When he wasn't in the air, he enjoyed the prayer meetings, formed strong friendships with some of the other pilots, and had a couple of regular carousing buddies who joined him in the search for female companionship in Manila. Still, for Stan, there was a troubling issue about squadron life, apart from the run-of-the-mill gripes they all shared. From time to time, he heard comments about Jews that he found infuriating. A flyer might talk about "Jewing someone down," or another would make a more overtly critical comment about Jews, only to be followed by the protestation that he had many Jewish friends. It was never anything major or, as he later wrote to Linden, it was "never anything you could poke a guy for."

In a short story titled "To All Concerned," Stan wrote about such an encounter, one in a line of seemingly minor yet maddening exposures to an anti-Semitic slur from a squadron-mate. In the story, Stan's fictional counterpart struggles with whether and how to respond, reflecting the turmoil that such experiences created in the real Stan. The main characters in "To All Concerned" are three pilots: Stone, Sam, and Carter. Stone, from whose point of view the story is told, is the squadron operations officer. He is Jewish, but secretly-so, having changed his last name and lacking a stereotypically "Jewish" appearance. Sam is also a Jew but is open about his affiliation and angry about the anti-Semitic slights he has encountered during his service. Carter is good-looking, clean-cut, and likable—an all-American boy.

Sam comes to Stone's tent for permission to go to Manila for Passover services. When Stone reveals that he too is Jewish, Sam is amazed, and then expresses his anger over the comments he has heard within the squadron, his frustration with the Jewish inclination to talk about anti-Semitism but do nothing about it, and his determination to fight the next time he hears a slur. Stone pushes back, questioning the usefulness of Sam's approach. Stone does not say it out loud but believes he has found the solution to anti-Semitism by hiding his Jewishness, something his gentile appearance and changed last name have allowed him to do.

Carter enters the tent as Sam leaves. The handsome young pilot is pleasant to the departing Sam but inwardly angry about a poker loss the night before. Once Sam is out of earshot, Carter turns to Stone and refers to Sam as a "lousy Jew bastard" and a "damm kike." In an instant, Stone is now confronted with the very issue that he and Sam had just argued about. Stone struggles internally over what to do next—to ignore the slight or to respond.

Stone ultimately decides to retaliate by assigning Carter, to the young pilot's obvious dismay, to a tough mission the next day that he was not scheduled to fly. But Stone never reveals his religion to Carter and does not explain the reason for his harsh action. As the story concludes, Stone knows that

he hasn't accomplished anything and that he will have to ultimately confront Carter. At the same time, Stone is consoled by
the fact that he has at least done something, that "[t]omorrow
that bastard flies."

Stan had inadvertently set himself up for the kind of incident that inspired "To All Concerned." Like the character in
the story, Stan's name change exposed him to comments he
might not have heard had the speaker been aware that he was
in the company of a Jew. The actor Kirk Douglas (born Issur
Danielovitch) once wrote that in the first years after changing
his name, he regularly found himself among people who did
not know that he was Jewish and listening to "things that in
their nightmares Jews speculate non-Jews say, and that I found
out, they do."

To be sure, Stan had a conflicted relationship with his
Jewishness. As if the name change alone was not enough, he
actively concealed his religion at times. In 2006, Jeff tracked
down Syl Mawrence, a former tentmate of Stan's in San
Marcelino. After Jeff introduced himself and explained that he
was writing a book about Stan, Syl's unexpected first words in
response were: "Look, I'm Jewish." He continued, clearly nurs-
ing a long-simmering hurt: "He [Stan] wouldn't admit to me
that he was Jewish." Mawrence explained that he thought Stan
was a fellow Jew and dropped a number of non-subtle hints
that Syl himself was Jewish, but Stan wouldn't bite, saying only
that he was from New York.

The kind of discomfort that Stan had experienced before
his name change reflected his deeper ambivalence about his
identity—his feeling that it was not really what primarily
defined who he was as a person. That ambivalence continued

during the war, as evidenced by his interactions with Syl Mawrence, someone to whom Stan could have disclosed his Jewishness without any fear of a hostile reaction. But, like many other Jewish soldiers during the war years, Stan's careful distancing from the religion of his parents ran headlong into the challenge of anti-Semitism. As Deborah Moore wrote in *GI Jews: How World War II Changed a Generation*: "No etiquette book guided Jews in responding to anti-Semitism. Each individual Jew had to decide how to react. Jews knew which words hurt and what behavior threatened them. But what, if anything, a man should do about it was less clear. The problem was far from abstract; it was deeply personal."

It seemed that nearly all Jewish GIs had a story to tell. Some faced overt anti-Semitism, including physical threats, while for others it might have been slurs of the kind portrayed in "To All Concerned." Some Jews accepted the situation quietly, not wanting to make trouble and hoping to fit in; others fought back with words; and still others physically confronted their tormentors. Stan had been one of the quiet ones but, as "To All Concerned" reflected, the emotional scars from such encounters were deep.

"To All Concerned" would become Stan's defining piece of writing at UCLA. As he put the finishing touches on it and submitted it to his short story class, he thought it had a good chance to be published. The professor read it aloud and the students discussed it. Their reaction was unanimous. Although they thought the story was well constructed, they were firmly opposed to seeing it in any literary journal. Rather than help counter anti-Semitism, they believed it would have precisely the opposite effect.

Stan was stunned by the class' reaction. In a long letter to Is, he wrote: "It never occurred to me that any one would think that Stone's action was reprehensible. And yet everyone did." He defended the story, explaining that he was trying to show what happens when "a man who is subconsciously ashamed of being Jewish, or afraid of it" is pushed so far that he finally must make a choice. And there was no doubt in his mind which choice the character had to make: "I tried to point out, both in the character of Sam, and in Stone, that the Jews must fight back, that they have rationalized, excused, apologized, and talked too long."

He tried to address the criticisms of his fellow students while preserving the essence of the story he wanted to tell. He made four major revisions, building up Sam's character, for example, to no avail. His peers still rejected it. Stan, however, was unrepentant. He passionately believed in the essential message of "To All Concerned"—that Jews had long excused anti-Semitism and the time had come to fight back. Clearly Stone *was* Stan, a Jew who often went unrecognized because of his physical appearance and name change, who had long rationalized a flight from his Jewishness, and who had been driven to reclaim his identity by an accumulation of seemingly minor encounters with anti-Semitism.

Chapter Nine

NEW RELATIONSHIPS

As I see it, we're in the backwash of the war boom now.
The tide is running out fast. Next year, in my opinion,
we'll see widespread depression and unemployment.
—The Best Years of Our Lives (1946)

Near the beginning of 1947, at the UCLA campus, Stan met Bob Vickman for the first time. For Bob, there had been no real question about where he was heading after the war. Los Angeles was the only city he had ever called home. His parents and brothers lived there and Vickman's, the family's restaurant, was a local fixture.

Bob had volunteered for the Army Air Corps and, like Stan, had dreamed of becoming a fighter pilot. He came close—an assignment to a P-38 squadron. The P-38 Lightning was the type of aircraft flown by America's "Ace of Aces,"

Richard Bong, who recorded forty kills in the Asian theater. But the planes in Bob's squadron were the F-5E, an unarmed, reconnaissance version of the revered fighter. He was assigned to the Pacific theater and flew more than fifty missions photographing Japanese positions, earning an Air Medal. Still, he had not been fully satisfied by his wartime service. As the squadron's official history put it: "Just to take a Jap's picture, was not a fighting man's idea of winning the war." Returning home from the Pacific, these were Bob's sentiments as well.

Stan and Bob had much in common. Both were artists. Like Stan, Bob also favored realistic works. In Bob's case, inspired by his childhood pastime of riding in the Los Angeles Hills with his brothers, he had a special fondness for painting horses. And yet Bob, like Stan, could occasionally be pulled in the direction of more whimsical, more abstract, subjects. Each man also had his pilot's wings. Both served in the Pacific and spent time on many of the same islands, even overlapping for a bit in the Philippines. Each man also had a wartime dream they had chased but not achieved—to fly fighters.

In addition, each had grown up in houses that were Jewish in the most nominal sense only. Neither had celebrated a bar mitzvah nor had any real connection with organized Jewish observance. Though Bob's mother was born in America, his father, like Stan's, had emigrated from Russia while still a teenager. Each, therefore, possessed, in addition to the sense of otherness that came from being Jewish in 1940s America, the sensibility of being the child of an immigrant.

Still, what brought the two together was their contrasts as much as their similarities. Stan's outgoing personality and easy manner with women were a source of amusement to Bob, who was much more reserved. Stan loved to tell dirty jokes, while Bob found it hard to swear even in the privacy of the journal that he kept throughout his time in the Pacific. Stan was the brash New Yorker, while Bob was the sober product of a Los Angeles that still had a rural feel and that had not yet found itself as a place that people went to reinvent themselves. For his part, Stan admired the way that the six-foot-three Bob weighed his words carefully, speaking little but always meaning what he said. They quickly became close friends, with Stan becoming a fixture at Sunday night dinners at the home of the close-knit Vickman family.

Always a faithful correspondent, Stan never failed to keep Linden informed about life in California or to encourage his friend to also make the move out west. The selection of UCLA had been a good one, and Stan was enjoying Los Angeles. But despite the city's wide-open reputation, his prowling days were in the past. Virginia Carvel had changed all of that.

Stan was drawn to Virginia from the beginning. She was tall and slender, with light brown hair worn loosely around her face. Like Stan, she was one of the older students on campus. A native of San Antonio, she had been a member of the WAVES during the war, instructing student pilots on a flight simulator known as a link trainer. She had loved her time in the military—the freedom, the independence, the friendship, and the adventurous spirit of the student pilots.

Her heart in those days did not belong to any of the handsome flyers that she trained, however. She was waiting for her high school sweetheart, Waylon, who was stationed overseas. A talented artist with a sensitive soul, he was devoted to her. One year, on Virginia's birthday, Waylon sent flowers to her mother, as thanks for bringing her daughter into the world. When Waylon failed to make it back from the war, Virginia had been devastated.

Stan reminded her of the fun-loving pilots she had known during her time in the WAVES. It wasn't long before their relationship became serious and Virginia started to envision a life together. Stan introduced her to Finley, who liked her instantly. When Linden came for a visit, he was soon urging his friend to propose. Stan liked everything about Virginia. Beyond her obvious good looks, he loved how she spoke with intelligence and assurance. He admired that she could be both reserved and poised. And it didn't hurt that Virginia was an art lover too, studying interior design. Still, having run around with so many girls, he wondered if he was capable of sticking with just one.

Sensing his deep-seated ambivalence, Virginia told Stan she couldn't see him anymore. He tried to dissuade her from breaking up but she held firm and the relationship appeared over. Then after several weeks, Virginia called Stan out of the blue, and they picked up where they left off. He continued to resist the idea of marriage, but he was overjoyed to be a couple again. One thing that had not held Stan back in his relationship with Virginia was that she was not Jewish. Stan's religion did, however, trouble Virginia's parents, a real-life playing out of *Earth and High Heaven*, Gwethalyn Graham's novel about the romance of a Jewish lawyer and a Protestant socialite against a backdrop of Canadian anti-Semitism, which had reached the top of the *New York Times'* bestseller list in 1944.

It was only a matter of time before Stan asked his girl-friend to sit for an oil portrait. He positioned her in profile, head slightly turned toward Stan, hair up. The finished product showed off his talent as a realistic artist, presenting Virginia's face in exquisite detail and reproducing, with nearly photographic precision, the animal design on her dress. Although the painting was a gift to Virginia, Stan considered asking for permission to hang it in a gallery, where it would be an advertisement for commission portraits. By then he had realized that the Warner Brothers job was not going to happen, and he was looking for other ways to earn money as an artist. He put together a portfolio and made the rounds of art services and advertising agencies. He gained nothing for his efforts. "I never received so many compliments and so few offers of jobs," he complained to Linden. "There isn't a bit of news, good or otherwise, as far as a job is concerned."

Stan's failure to find work—a common struggle in a workforce that was facing the twin pressures of laid-off defense workers and returning veterans clamoring for jobs—was becoming an increasing source of concern. Though he, like all vets, was entitled to a twenty-dollar weekly allotment in his first year as a civilian, his membership in the "52-20 Club," as the benefit had become known, was set to expire. As he wrote to Linden: "[M]y bank balance is fast dwindling. As far as I'm concerned, the much-heralded depression is already here. Jobs are as scarce as the proverbial pullet's dentures."

Stan was also concerned about a different drama—one that was playing out in the newspapers in late 1947. Republicans in Congress were intensifying their efforts to substantiate allegations of Communist infiltration of the government and private sector, including the movie business. Operating through the House Un-American Activities Committee

(HUAC), their ire focused on pro-Soviet movies that had been released during the war, while the U.S. and Russia were allies in the fight against Hitler.

The hearings began in Washington on October 20, 1947, and Stan followed them closely, disgusted by the so-called Communism "experts" who testified before the Committee. He could see that the HUAC members did not care whether their charges were true. Yet, he understood that the Committee could not be blithely dismissed. Anti-Red hysteria was a real and growing phenomenon. e He As he devoted more of his creative energy to exploring anti-Semitism, he was also struck by the growing equation in the public mind between Jews and Communism. To many, one was a synonym for the other.

The HUAC hearings were not the only news story that captured Stan's attention, interrupting an otherwise idyllic beginning to his new life in Los Angeles. There was also the issue of Palestine.

Chapter Ten

PALESTINE

For some time now, I have been engaged upon a work of indescribable greatness. I do not know yet whether I shall carry it through. It has assumed the aspect of some mighty dream.
—Theodor Herzl, *The Jewish State* (1896)

In 1895, a Viennese journalist named Theodor Herzl, despairing of a Jewish future in a Europe that was marked by persistent anti-Semitic attitudes, wrote *The Jewish State*. In it, he advocated a return to Zion after two thousand years of exile as the solution to the problem of long-term Jewish security in a gentile world. Previously, such notions had been the stuff of messianic dreams.

Herzl had been a secular and indifferent Jew, at one point even arguing for mass baptism as a solution to the problem of anti-Semitism. Over time, though, he came to think that nothing could guarantee the acceptance of Europe's Jews, including conversion to Christianity. Like Stan, Herzl initially sought a fictional outlet for his thoughts. In a play called *The New Ghetto*, Herzl's Jewish protagonist dies in a duel with an anti-Semitic tormentor. His book *The Jewish State*, setting forth a program for a Jewish return to Zion, followed a few years later.

Herzl's brand of political Zionism slowly won believers, particularly among the oppressed Jews of Russia. Immigration to Palestine surged in the early years of the twentieth century. In 1917, as World War I raged, Great Britain issued what came to be known as the "Balfour Declaration," which viewed "with favor" the establishment of a Jewish homeland in Palestine, then ruled by the Ottoman Turks, one of England's wartime adversaries. In 1921, following the Allied victory in the war and the dissolution of the Ottoman Empire, the League of Nations granted England a mandate to establish a Jewish state. But recurring Arab violence throughout the 1920s and 1930s led to a progressive weakening of Britain's commitment. In response to the Arab "revolt" of 1936–1939, England issued the White Paper of 1939 that put limits on Jewish immigration and land purchases in a futile effort to assuage Arab anger— and to also assure continued access to Middle Eastern oil supplies. As a result, throughout the war years, Palestine's doors were virtually sealed to Jews seeking to flee the Nazis.

The America that had beckoned immigrants to its shores at the time that Stan's parents arrived at Ellis Island had also not been a savior for European Jews. Attitudes toward immigrants generally, and Jewish immigrants, in particular, had hardened after the end of World War I. The early 1920s saw the passage of a series of restrictive immigration laws that made it increasingly difficult for Jews fleeing Russia or parts of Europe to enter. Economic fears of an invasion of foreign workers during the Depression, amplified by organized labor groups that had been a bastion for the Jews of Stan's parents' generation, fueled a determination to keep the immigration doors firmly shut during the 1930s when frightened German and other European Jews most needed an escape. All of that, coupled with an ingrained anti-Semitism in the ranks of State Department diplomats, ensured that the U.S. would not become a refuge for Europe's Jews either before or during the war years. With the news of the extent of the decimation of European Jewry emerging in the weeks and months following Germany's surrender, it also became clear to many in the American Jewish community, Stan among them, of the extent to which U.S. immigration policy had contributed to the destruction.

There was, for American Jews, the added recognition that their failure to more forcefully advocate on behalf of their European brethren also contributed to the magnitude of the destruction. There was little doubt that Jewish wartime silence was the product of fear and a sense of not fully belonging, of not being complete American citizens. There had been Charles Lindbergh's incendiary charge during his campaign against U.S. involvement in the war in Europe that the Jews did not truly have American interests at heart.[4] That charge, combined with persistent anti-Semitism throughout society and lingering

---

[4] Lindbergh, who little more than a decade earlier had become the first person to fly across the Atlantic Ocean, became the leading face of the forces resisting American entry into a second European war under the banner of a campaign entitled "America First." The delegitimization of Jewish support for an aggressive anti-Germany policy reached its zenith in a speech that Lindbergh gave in Iowa in September of 1941, three months before Pearl Harbor. There he attacked the Jews directly, declaring that "[t]heir greatest danger to this country lies in their large ownership and influence in our motion pictures, our press, our radio, and our government."

questions about Jewish patriotism, almost completely muzzled American Jews during the late 1930s and throughout the war. By 1943, American Jewish groups had begun to finally rally around the idea that Palestine's doors should be open to Jewish refugees, but the idea that *America's* doors should be pried loose was one that had little organized Jewish support.

That same fear, that anxiety about what other Americans might think, also explained much of the mainstream Jewish community's ambivalence toward the unfolding Zionist enterprise in Palestine. While the logic of Palestine as a Jewish refuge gained increasingly greater acceptance, the idea of it becoming an independent Jewish state was less universally shared. The American Jewish Committee, one of the oldest and most respected Jewish organizations, continued to oppose full Jewish statehood throughout the war years.

With Lindbergh's anti-Semitism-tinged isolationism thoroughly discredited by Pearl Harbor and swamped by an irreversible tide of wartime fervor, things started to change. American Jewish service in all branches of the military—over the course of the war, five hundred fifty thousand American Jews wore a uniform—quelled most doubts about a Jewish willingness to fight for America, except among the most committed anti-Semites. For individual Jewish servicemen like Stan and Bob, service in the war profoundly changed their image of themselves and their place in the country, giving them confidence as Americans that their parents were never able to fully experience. It also provided them with a lesser willingness than their parents' generation to tolerate anti-Semitism.

Starting in late 1945, news of the Holocaust refocused international attention on Palestine. With the war over, hundreds of thousands of Jewish refugees languished in displaced persons (DP) camps in Europe. Returning to homes in an annihilated community in an unrepentantly anti-Semitic Poland was not an option that many were willing to consider. To most, Europe was now a graveyard. America, despite increasing public sympathy for the plight of the Jews, remained uninterested in opening the immigration floodgates, particularly with millions of returning servicemen and the staggering loss of defense jobs already threatening the postwar economic recovery. That left Palestine as the most logical choice for resettlement.

Working through the Haganah, a paramilitary group established to defend the Jews against Arab attacks, Palestinian Jews organized a high-profile campaign to draw the world's attention to the British naval blockade that kept DPs from entering the country. The Haganah purchased war-surplus ships from the U.S., hired predominantly American crews to operate them, and sailed the hastily refurbished vessels to France. There, it loaded thousands of Jewish refugees for the cramped and perilous voyage to Palestine. As each boat approached Palestine's territorial waters, the British would forcibly board it and imprison the refugees in camps in Cyprus. Each boarding created more sympathy for the cause of Jewish statehood. This campaign, which continued from 1946 to the end of 1947, came to be known as "Aliyah Bet," the Second Immigration.[5]

The most famous of the Aliyah Bet ships was the President Warfield, a luxury steamer that for years had ferried

---

[5]   The name Aliyah Bet was intended to distinguish it from the limited legal immigration permitted by the British, or "Aliyah Aleph," the First Immigration.

passengers back and forth across Maryland's Chesapeake Bay. Filled to more than ten times its original capacity with refugees crammed into hastily-constructed bunks, it sailed from France on July 9, 1947. For the last leg of the journey, it carried a new name, *Exodus 1947*. A flotilla of British warships intercepted the *Exodus* as it approached Palestinian waters. The captain tried to slip past them so that he could beach on Palestine's shores, but the overloaded steamer was no match for the military vessels that surrounded it. The Brits rammed the refugee ship from both sides, knocking huge holes above the waterline. Dozens of Royal Marines then leaped onto the deck from the neighboring warships, surging past flying cans of food and other debris thrown by the desperate and otherwise unarmed passengers, to take control of the wheelhouse. In the ensuing melee, the boarding party killed an American seaman and one of the teenage passengers.

Not satisfied with the successful capture of the vessel, Britain's Foreign Secretary Ernest Bevin felt that something dramatic needed to be done to dissuade any further attempts at breaking the blockade. After setting foot on Palestinian soil only long enough to leave the *Exodus* and board one of three prison ships, the refugees were shipped off to the British zone of occupation in Germany. By the time the passengers finally disembarked, England was dealing with an unmitigated public relations disaster.

The saga of the *Exodus* riveted the American public. Newsreel cameras had captured the towing of the battered ship into Haifa harbor and the loading of her bedraggled passengers onto the prison vessels. The story even found its way into UCLA's *Daily Bruin*, a school paper that was more typically concerned with the fortunes of the football team and the latest fashion trends. To further galvanize public opinion, the Haganah sent some members of the *Exodus'* crew to the U.S. on a multi-city speaking tour. On October 9, 1947, one of them spoke at UCLA.

Through the winter of 1947, Palestine remained on the front pages of America's newspapers. Fighting between Jews and Arabs intensified. Britain, still reeling economically from World War II and unable to find a formula for reconciling competing Arab and Jewish claims, just wanted to get out. In April, it turned the problem over to the United Nations General Assembly. The U.N. appointed a commission of inquiry—the United Nations Special Committee on Palestine (UNSCOP)—to investigate conditions and propose a solution. In August, UNSCOP recommended that the land be partitioned into separate Jewish and Arab states. On November 29, 1947, following intense politicking and with the support of both the United States and Russia, the U.N. General Assembly endorsed partition by a vote of thirty-three to thirteen, barely breaking the two-thirds majority needed for passage. Britain accepted the decision and set May 15, 1948, as its departure date from Palestine.

The vote, though, solved little. While the Jews exulted in the partition vote, literally dancing in the streets in celebration, the Arab countries remained bitterly opposed to the idea of a Jewish state in their midst. In Palestine, attacks on outlying Jewish settlements, sniping along the roads, and the infiltration of irregular soldiers intensified. The leaders of the neighboring states—Egypt, Jordan, Syria, and Lebanon—spoke openly of using armed force to block the partition. In the weeks and months following the historic U.N. vote, it became clear that a Jewish homeland would only be established by armed force. To defeat the Arabs, the Jews would need to build an army.

Chapter Eleven

FIGHTING BACK

There's a funny kind of elation about socking back.
    —*Gentleman's Agreement* (1947)

A s Stan and Bob got to know each other better, exchanging views on art, politics, and flying, they soon discovered that Palestine was another area of common interest. Both men had become convinced that the Jews had a right to a state and that they would need to fight to get it. They also recognized that what was playing out in Palestine was historic—an opportunity for the Jews, a people so long victimized by anti-Semitism, to fight back against their oppressors and finally take control of their destiny. The two began to discuss whether there was a role that they, as former combat pilots, might be able to play in the struggle.

They were not alone; among Jewish veterans, newly-emboldened by their wartime service, there was now strong sympathy for the Zionist enterprise. On July 16, 1946, four thousand of them marched in Washington in support of an American proposal to immediately allow one hundred thousand Jewish refugees to enter Palestine, an initiative firmly opposed by Britain. Representatives of the group announced that if American troops were needed to facilitate the entry of the displaced Jews, they would recruit "a full division of Jewish volunteers for service in the Holy Land."

But an announcement by the State Department that passports would not be issued to men seeking to travel to the Middle East to fight put a quick end to such grand ideas. Few Americans, however motivated, were prepared to openly flout their government and risk the loss of citizenship. The State Department ban ended the open recruitment for a Jewish army, but the effort continued underground, led by the Haganah. The organization was primarily interested in airmen. While a highly motivated recruit could be quickly trained to fire a rifle and placed into the infantry, there was no real shortcut to learning to fly. That meant that pilots for a Jewish air force would have to arrive fully trained. In October 1947, Aharon Remez and Hyman Shamir, two influential members of the Haganah who had served in western air forces during World War II, developed a blueprint for a Jewish air force that would fly predominantly war-surplus planes from America, with crews recruited in the U.S.

An additional roadblock in front of the Remez/Shamir plan was that President Harry Truman's administration firmly opposed weapons sales to the Jews, particularly planes. On

March 26, 1948, the President issued Proclamation 2776, expanding the list of materials that would be regarded as military and that would require State Department approval for export to effectively include all aircraft. That restriction was scheduled to enter into effect on April 15. That action and the ban on the participation of American citizens in the Palestinian conflict seemed to effectively scuttle the Remez/Shamir vision of an air force based on American crewmen flying U.S.-made, war-surplus planes.

The Haganah quickly adjusted to this new reality. With open recruitment of volunteers impossible, it established a front group—Land and Labor for Palestine—to conceal its attempts to find American veterans willing to go to Palestine. A second Haganah front, Materials for Palestine, masked the search for war-surplus weapons on U.S. soil. The companies set up shop in Manhattan at the Hotel Fourteen on East 60th Street, the owners of which were sympathetic to the cause. The address was best known as the home of the Copacabana, the famed New York nightspot located in the hotel's basement.

Despite the State Department's travel ban, a number of American Jews found a way to get involved in the effort to establish a Jewish air force. One of the most important was Al Schwimmer, a TWA flight engineer and veteran transport pilot. Between December 1947 and February 1948, Schwimmer led the search for flight and ground crews and also supervised the purchase of ten Curtiss Commandos and three Lockheed Constellations on the war-surplus market. The Curtiss Commando, more popularly known as the C-46, was one of the largest twin-engine planes ever manufactured. The reliable transport craft had been the backbone of the Allied effort to move supplies over the Hump to troops in Burma. The four-engine Constellation had even greater capacity and range.

Through a complicated series of moves that involved both a dummy American airline and a fake Panamanian one, Schwimmer arranged for the aircraft to be smuggled to South America before President Truman's export ban went into effect. By mid-April 1948, the planes were assembled at Tocumen Airport in Panama City, where they made up the fleet of Lineas Aereas de Panama, Sociedad Anonima (LAPSA), ostensibly Panama's new national airline.

Schwimmer's operation provided the Palestinian Jews with an air transport arm, but he could not figure out how to procure American planes with offensive military capacity. So as 1948 began and events in Palestine surged inexorably toward war, the search for fighters and bombers moved beyond the States. There was no shortage of leads—P-40s and B-25s in Mexico, Spitfires in England and France, Macchis in Italy. Representatives of the Haganah chased down each rumor, but, time and again, could not close a deal. Still, the Haganah believed that fighter planes would turn up sooner or later, and Land and Labor wanted to be ready with trained flyers when they did.

There was an improvisational nature to Land and Labor's recruitment in the U.S. Jewish veterans who were known as experienced pilots might find themselves recruited directly. Other times, though, it was the pilot who sought out the opportunity. That was how Stan and Bob got involved. Discreet inquiries led the two pilots to a Los Angeles representative of Land and Labor, and in April 1948, they received a phone call, summoning them to an after-hours meeting at a local office building the next day. When the two arrived, they found four other men, also flyers, who were there for the same reason. One by one, the six pilots were summoned to an inner room, where two men in business suits questioned them about their background, military training, and motivation, dutifully recording the answers on a form. Stan and Bob were each given a doctor's name and instructed to make an appointment for a physical and a series of shots. After all six were interviewed, the men in suits gathered everyone together and told them to keep quiet about everything they had just experienced.

As Stan and Bob made their way through the screening process, the Haganah still had no combat aircraft for them to fly. It certainly didn't have any B-25s or P-38s, and there was no expectation that these two Americans would be flying in Palestine the same types of planes they had flown for the U.S. during the war. But, for the two UCLA students, that was part of the attraction. They would not be cheated a second time. This time, Land and Labor assured them, they would get the chance to fly fighters.

As he confided in a letter to his WWII tentmate, Bob felt that having given several years to Uncle Sam during the war, he could give a few months to his people to help them get their own state. For Stan, it was more complicated. Though confessing to a "certain amount of idealism," he did not think of himself as a Zionist. As he wrote to Linden: "Personally, I don't give a damn about Zionism. Theoretically, as a matter of fact, I think it's harmful. I'd rather see Jews assimilate into all nations, rather than setting up a separate racial culture. So it's not for that reason that I'd be sticking my neck out."

Rather, as Stan saw it, the Jews of Palestine, at long last, were striking back against the anti-Semites, and he wanted to have a part in the fight. He had finally found a way to address the issue that had stirred him since his time in the air corps, the one he had spent so much energy probing in the many versions of "To All Concerned." He described his thinking to Linden: "For some time—since I entered the army, in fact, I've been increasingly troubled about anti-Semitism, and the problems of being a Jew, no matter how atheistic, in a Christian world. Not being religious I had never considered myself a Jew, except by accident. I find, however, that the label is forced on me, whether I like it or not. And now, out of perversity perhaps, I refuse to discard it, even if I have a chance—and I definitely do, not looking, talking, or acting what is popularly conceived as being Jewish.

"Merely admitting or even proclaiming loudly one's Jewishness these days is not enough, however. For one of the few times in history, there seems to be a definite opportunity to get in a few licks in the fight. The Jew has always been known as an intellectual, not a fighter, a turner of cheeks, a beggar for help against oppression, always the victim, never the victor. Every time there is an outbreak of anti-Semitism, a pogrom, or an organized campaign of extinction, what have the Jews done—passed resolutions, sent petitions, wrote letters, made speeches—and never fought. That can be pretty frustrating, and a hell of a label to carry around with you. If, then, we can fight back, just once, I intend to do it."

Stan sent a similar letter to his older brother, the one that Craig would read more than sixty years later in Libby Anekstein's apartment. Is was the only family member to whom

Stan was prepared to reveal his plans. In addition to explaining his idealistic reasons for going, Stan also told Is about a more practical aspect of the looming adventure. He and Bob recognized the historical significance of what was going on in Palestine and knew they would have a front-row seat for the action. With Bob's skill as a photographer and Stan's as a writer—not to mention both of their backgrounds as artists—they were ideally suited to capture the struggle in every artistic medium. Stan told Is that they had built a special box and loaded it with their "tools," including a still camera and enough film to take three thousand five hundred pictures; a movie camera and ten thousand feet of film; a typewriter; paints; brushes and paper.

Stan explained that he also planned to contact the *New York Post*'s foreign editor Johannes Steel and a literary agent before leaving the country, hoping to arrange to sell articles about his experiences in Palestine.[6] "This, of course, will serve a double purpose, or rather triple—I can turn out propaganda for the Jews, make money, and also a name for myself with publishers and agents. And I really think articles like that will find a ready market—you know—'I Fly For The Haganah!!!!' and stuff like that." He believed the movies, as well, would be valuable, as a visual aid for lectures he could give Jewish groups once he returned. Finally, he would be able to "gather excellent material" for a book about his experience.

Stan was convinced that at least one of these creative endeavors would work out after the fighting was over, but

---

[6] Steel had established himself as a shrewd analyst of world affairs when he published a book in 1934 that predicted a second world war. Later, he predicted the Japanese attack on Pearl Harbor one week before it occurred.

that did not, in his view, lessen the "idealistic aspect of it." He assured Is that "I'd do it even if there were nothing in it for me, but there's no reason why I can't combine both, so long as one doesn't harm the other."

Stan knew his brother would be opposed to the whole enterprise, so he tried to anticipate the objections that were certain to come his way. Is would worry about the effect on Joseph and Rebecca, who had already lived under the stress of having two sons away at war. Their parents would not worry, assured Stan, because he would not tell them of his real plans. While he would disclose that he was going to Palestine, he would leave out the part about flying. Instead, Stan would only tell them that he was going to write magazine articles and gather material for a book, both of which were partially true.

Is would also worry about his younger brother getting into trouble with the U.S. military or State Department. "Well, that's tough. I'll have to take my chances," Stan explained. "On my passport application I'll say I'm going to Europe to get material for a book. On my Reserve Change of Address form I'll say the same thing. I see no reason why they should ever find out, but if they do, well, as I said, that's tough. If there's a National Emergency and Reserve Officers are called up, I'll report to the Consulate for duty." There was another reason why Stan was not concerned about the U.S. government. "As melodramatic as it may sound," he wrote Is, "I'll probably be operating under a pseudonym."

Stan's letter was not meant to sidestep a confrontation with his brother over what was clearly a momentous decision. He invited Is, who was living in Michigan, to come to New York so they could thoroughly talk things through before Stan left the country. At the same time, Stan didn't want there to be any sense that his decision was reversible. "I'm quite serious about this thing, Is, and it's not just a sudden whim, or even an escape from boredom and unsatisfying progress here, although I'd be lying if I said there were no traces of those factors in my reasons for going. I insist, however, that those are minor considerations. I'm going because I think I should, because I want to, and because I must. And when I'm there I intend to make the most of it, in every way. I hope you agree with me, but whether you do or not, I'm going," he wrote. Undeterred by the firmness of Stan's tone, Is agreed to make the trip east.

There was one complication Stan had not discussed with Is. Stan did not want to leave Virginia and that part of the decision weighed on him. She was distraught when he told her of his plans and not simply because she had already lost one boyfriend in war. She had continued to hope for a future together and Stan's decision now threatened all of that.

But whether Virginia understood or not, Stan simply had to go. When he thought of what he and Bob were proposing to do, he did not see any negatives. There would be the opportunity to fight back against anti-Semitism. His experiences might give him the material for a book, allowing him to realize his ambition of becoming a writer. Or perhaps the photography or filming would turn into something. He felt that he would "come out of this thing a big man, both materially and mentally," and he was determined to give himself every chance to do that. Going to Palestine, he believed, was "the big opportunity in my life."

Chapter Twelve

SEEING THE SITES

Spring is coming; spring is coming; our blood runs quicker;
active service is within measurable distance; and the future
beckons to us with both hands to step down at last into
the arena, and try our fortune amid the uncertain but
illimitable chances of the greatest game in the World.
—Ian Hay (John Hay Beith),
The First Hundred Thousand (1915)

n April, Stan and Bob received notice from Land and Labor that it was time to head out. They were given airline tickets to New York and the address of an office in Manhattan that would be their first stop. Bob's brothers and parents accompanied him to the airport. As with Stan's family, all but one of the members of Bob's family (in his case it was his older brother Harry) were in the dark about the real nature of the trip. Still, they knew enough about the situation in Palestine to fear for his safety, and the separation was a sad one.

In New York, Stan and Bob arrived at the offices of Service Airways, a made-up airline that held title to Schwimmer's fleet of transport planes. The bustling office was littered with aviation paraphernalia—maps, logbooks, and telegraphy equipment. A man holding their completed interview forms from Los Angeles instructed the pair of pilots to apply immediately for passports because they would be taking a commercial flight to Europe in a week or so.

They traveled down to Washington to take care of the passports. The application asked them to explain the reason for their trip. Disclosing the truth was obviously out of the question, so they wrote that they were traveling to Italy and France to gather historical and background material for an independent movie to be produced in New York and Los Angeles. Stan put down that he was a writer, while Bob presented himself as a filmmaker. They got the passports without incident and returned to New York to wait.

A few days later, Stan and Is had their get-together. Is found himself in an awkward position—part brother, part father. He tried to talk Stan out of going, fulfilling the role that his parents would have played had they been privy to the secret. Back and forth it went, Is making his arguments and Stan deflecting them. As he had made clear in the letter, Stan's mind was made up. If you are determined to go, a defeated Is finally offered, "you have my blessing."

For Stan, there was one more reunion to come. With Bob along for the ride, he headed to New Jersey to visit Esther. He told her they were going to Palestine but little else, and though she had her suspicions, Esther didn't press for more information. She was just happy to have some time with the baby brother she had not seen since he moved to California more than a year and a half earlier.

One afternoon back in New York, in a scene out of the popular wartime novel *Shore Leave* about carousing soldiers on R&R in San Francisco, Stan and Bob threw a lively party in their room at the Windsor Hotel. The alcohol flowed freely, and the guests included a pretty young blonde. In the midst of the festivities, someone raced in to announce that the hotel was being raided. It was the FBI, apparently on the trail of Land and Labor's Palestine recruits. The Feds grabbed a radio operator, but everyone else made it out safely. Stan and Bob moved to another hotel to continue the wait.

At last, it was time to leave. On May 5, they jumped into a cab bound for the airport to catch an Air France flight to Paris. Though they didn't know what was coming next, Stan was not looking too far ahead. The flight itself—a luxurious affair with excellent food, wine, and champagne—provided more than its share of diversions. Stan spotted Marilyn Buferd, Miss America, 1946. Ever the brash one, he did not hesitate to approach her. They shared a home state and a college; Buferd had won her Miss California title while a student at UCLA. Like Stan, she was leaving the States behind for the foreseeable future. She was on her way back to Europe, where she had been studying languages at the University of Berlitz and modeling prototype bikinis on the runways of Paris. They made plans to get together in France.

Another passenger was George "Buzz" Beurling, a Canadian, who was also on his way to join the Jewish air force.

Unlike Stan and Bob, however, Beurling was far from a new-comer to fighters. During World War II, the Canadian had been his country's leading ace, recording thirty-one and a third kills over Malta, an astounding twenty-seven of them in a single two-week period. His exploits had earned him the nickname "The Falcon of Malta." Stan and Bob could not have chosen a better travel companion than Beurling, given what they were on their way to do. The Canadian was known for being generous with his military knowledge, including his legendary, if somewhat unorthodox, training methods.[7]

At the airport in Paris, it appeared for a moment that their trip might come to an abrupt end. The French police closely inspected the group's passports, talking animatedly among themselves for almost an hour before letting the flyers enter the country. Though Land and Labor quickly shuttled the group of volunteers to Rome, the lengthy inspection at the border had made everyone nervous.

The stay in Rome lasted ten days and the men made the most of it. Put up in a swanky hotel, they walked the city during the day and hit the clubs at night. Bob made two trips to the Vatican, including an extended visit to the Sistine Chapel where he was able to see in person works by Michelangelo that he had long admired from his classroom studies. As Stan described it to Linden, they ate like kings, drank wine by the gallon, bought all sorts of souvenirs, and went everywhere by taxi—without paying a cent. Land and Labor took care of it all.

---

[7] These included, when Beurling had been stationed on Malta, hunting lizards with a .38 pistol at a distance that he felt simulated the challenge of shooting down a Messerschmitt at the range typically encountered during a dogfight.

These were young men going to war and the pilots were particularly interested in the local women. Between them, they picked up an international set—women from Italy, France, Spain, Germany, Sweden, Rumania (now Romania), and Hungary—most of whom sang or danced at the clubs they passed through. Rome's nightlife was especially mesmerizing to Stan, who had spent World War II in one remote, female-free location after another. One morning at 2 a.m., he took a dancer to the Colosseum where they had sex. "It's great to see the sites," he quipped to Linden in a letter a few days later.

Postwar Rome was lively and exotic, though the traffic, Stan thought, would drive a New York or Los Angeles cop "stark, staring mad in half an hour." As he described the scene to Linden: "They drive these tiny little cars that Bob is crazy about, step on the gas around corners, drive on all sides of the street, left, right and crossways, have no lights at all, and seem absolutely determined to kill every pedestrian in the street." And yet, Stan had to admit, he hadn't seen a single accident.

He loved the outdoor cafés, where the guys could take in an outdoor concert as they watched the prostitutes looking for business around the Piazza. Everywhere were men in uniform though no two, it seemed, wore the same type. Small puppies were constantly underfoot but, oddly, no one ever seemed to see a grown dog.

One particularly enchanting evening, Stan and Bob joined a crowd that had gathered at the edge of a park around a blind accordion player sitting on a stone. The man played Beethoven and Brahms, and Bob, the better judge of music, deemed the playing beautiful. The number of spectators grew until some were standing in the street, oblivious to the cars that veered around them. The pilots couldn't help but think that in the States, a cop would have broken the whole thing up in just a few minutes for blocking traffic, if anyone even bothered to stop and listen in the first place.

Meanwhile, events in the Middle East continued toward a showdown. On May 14, 1948, David Ben-Gurion, the political leader of the Jewish community, officially declared Jewish independence in Palestine. "Israel" would be the name of the new state. President Truman followed almost immediately with an announcement of recognition. That did not stop Egypt from bombing Tel Aviv that very night—the long-expected war had begun. In Rome, the Land and Labor recruits watched the unfolding drama with frustration. Expecting to be there at the start, they were still a continent away.

They unleashed that frustration on the Palestinians—now Israelis—who were shepherding them through Rome. Stan dubbed them the "rear echelon chairborne," and he was particularly vocal in letting them know what he thought of them. "They think they're playing cops and robbers or something. What a bunch of dimwitted infants," he wrote Linden. As he reacclimated himself to military life, he was reminded of his dislike for "wheels."

To make matters worse, their planes, or "tools" as Stan had taken to calling them, were not ready. Though the pilots were assured that the aircraft had been purchased, the government had run into problems getting them to Israel. Though they did not yet know the whole story, they were beginning to get a sense of what the Israeli air force had in store for them. The Israelis had, in fact, finally found fighter planes they could buy.

But they were not going to be Spitfires, Mustangs, or any other frontline, Western fighter.

In the end, only Czechoslovakia (which split in 1993 into Slovakia and the Czech Republic [now Czechia]) had been willing to violate the U.S.-led embargo on weapons shipments to the Middle East. On May 5, an agreement was finalized for sale to Israel, of all things, of the German-designed Messerschmitt, the Me-109. As part of the deal, the Czechs agreed to provide conversion training for the new fighter pilots, none of whom had any experience with the German plane. That training would take place behind the Iron Curtain, at a base in Czechoslovakia. It was there, Stan and Bob and the others learned, that they were now headed.

On May 15, Stan received a ticket to fly from Rome to Paris, by way of Nice. Though he was traveling without many of the other pilots, Stan was assured that at least he and Bob would meet up again shortly. Arriving in Paris, he had a chance to call Marilyn Buferd to arrange the date they had talked about almost a month earlier on the flight from New York. He was disappointed to learn that she had left that morning for Deauville and would not return until the 17th. Stan would be leaving on the 16th, and their rendezvous in France was not to be.

Still, Stan made the most of his time in Paris. In the evening, he walked along the Champs-Élysées, with its charming cafés and smart shops. It was warm and the street was filled with people. It struck Stan that all the women looked beautiful. Maybe, he wrote to Linden, "It's the way they wear their clothes (on them the New Look looks terrific), maybe it's their hair, or the way they carry themselves, maybe it was just the propaganda that's always drilled into us, maybe it's because Spring was definitely in the air."

Later that night, Stan ran into some of the other pilots. They hit four clubs in quick succession getting "nicely drunk" in the process. It was the end of a memorable day. Stan had discovered the storied magic of the "City of Light" that he had never believed existed. It was, he thought, one of the most beautiful cities he had ever seen. When he left, it was with the certainty that he would be back again.

The next day, Stan boarded a train for Geneva, headed north toward Czechoslovakia. With no available space in any of the sleepers for the all-night trip, he made do in a first-class compartment, passing the time writing a long letter to his friends Linden and Finley.

Stan arrived in Geneva on the 17th and was met at the station by a group that included Bob. The two had a day to explore the Swiss city which Stan found to be charming, though far quieter than Paris. The next morning, they ate a pleasant breakfast on their hotel terrace, a mild breeze keeping the sun-drenched morning from becoming too hot. They sat and watched as a number of attractive local girls, blonde hair flowing, pedaled gracefully by on their bicycles. Zürich was next, which was an even quieter city than Geneva. The people there spoke German and Stan discovered that the small amount of Yiddish he had remembered from childhood allowed him to get along surprisingly well.

Stan wrote to his parents so they could see a Geneva postmark. Despite what he had told Is in April, he now decided not to tell them that he was going to Palestine at all. Lying to his family did not come easily, and he delicately skirted the truth, withholding critical information but abstaining from outright falsehoods: "Just a short note to tell you not to expect mail from me for about two weeks. I'll be traveling on a very interesting assignment." He cautioned that the return address "doesn't mean that I'm staying in Geneva. As a matter of fact, I'm there only rarely."

Zurich ended the sightseeing phase of their journey. After less than a day, they were on the move again, eventually reaching Czechoslovakia. While they were still more than one thousand eight hundred miles from Israel, they were finally going to get the chance to climb into the cockpit of a fighter.

Chapter Thirteen

FIGHTER PILOTS

From Stettin in the Baltic to Trieste in the Adriatic an iron curtain has descended across the Continent. Behind that line lie all the capitals of the ancient states of Central and Eastern Europe. Warsaw, Berlin, Prague, Vienna, Budapest, Belgrade, Bucharest and Sofia, all these famous cities and the populations around them lie in what I must call the Soviet sphere, and all are subject in one form or another, not only to Soviet influence but to a very high and, in some cases, increasing measure of control from Moscow.
—Winston Churchill, speech at Westminster
College, Fulton, Missouri (March 5, 1946)

Czechoslovakia in the spring of 1948 was on the Russian side of the Iron Curtain that separated Europe into Soviet and Western spheres of influence. As it happened, that worked to the advantage of the advocates for a Jewish state. For the Soviets, Israel was fertile ground for limiting British influence in the Middle East and, in so doing, further confronting the West. Spurred by this geopolitical calculus, Moscow gave Czechoslovakia the green light to sell weapons to the Jews.

Czechoslovakia was in a position to help because of the happenstance of a German military decision near the end of World War II. The country's Nazi occupiers had established a Messerschmitt production line at the Avia factory in Prague as part of an effort to disperse weapons facilities and save them from punishing Allied air attacks. The war ended before the plant could be utilized and the Czechs had inherited it, along with the parts to manufacture Me-109s.

Following an explosion in one of its factories, Avia no longer had any of the powerful Daimler-Benz DB 605 engines that had made the Messerschmitt the match of the best American fighters in the European theater. There were, however, a number of heavier and slower Jumo 211F engines which had powered Junkers Ju 88 bombers, and the Jumo happened to fit the engine compartment of a Me-109. Unfortunately, the new engine radically altered the plane's performance characteristics. It climbed far slower than the German original, and, more troubling, it had a tendency to veer sharply on takeoffs and landings, making it highly dangerous to fly. But the Israelis were in no position to complain. They needed fighters and the modified Me-109 was available. A Czech Jew named Otto Felix negotiated the purchase of ten planes and took an option on fifteen more.

Felix also negotiated for a pilot training course, to be conducted in English, by Czech veterans of the RAF at an air base near the town of České Budějovice. The Czechs also agreed to allow the Israelis the use of a second field, near the town of Žatec, to house the fleet of transport planes that Al Schwimmer had smuggled out of the U.S. From Žatec, the transport fleet could ferry a wide assortment of military hardware, including light and heavy guns and ammunition that Israel was also purchasing from the Communist country to an Israeli base called Ekron. All of this activity violated the Truman administration's embargo on the sale of weapons to the Middle East—a policy that the State Department fully expected all other countries to follow.

The planes and the bases solved a number of Israel's problems but not all of them. Žatec was nearly two thousand miles from Tel Aviv. The C-46s that were the backbone of the transport fleet could travel only one thousand seven hundred miles before requiring more fuel. Clearly, an intermediate base was necessary. As for the Messerschmitts, the situation was far worse. Their maximum range was two hundred fifty miles, so a flight to Israel would require more than seven stops along the way. It would be difficult enough to find one more country willing to turn a blind eye to Israel's violation of the weapons embargo. Finding another half dozen was going to be impossible.

Jewish operatives had been active in Europe for several years, and during that time they had managed to gain access to one airfield in Italy and another in Corsica. A failed C-46 landing in March at the Italian strip, a short one in Perugia, eliminated it from consideration. An arrangement was instead made with the manager of the Corsican field and transport flights between Žatec and Israel, by way of the Corsican town of Ajaccio, which commenced shortly before Israel's declaration of independence.

In early May, a solution was also found to the problem of transporting the Messerschmitts. An Israeli named Pinchas Ben-Porat discovered that if the fighter was separated into sections, it was possible to fit the parts through the cargo doors of a C-46, with the body traveling in one plane and the wings, propeller, and bomb load in another. The sections would be reassembled in Israel with help from Czech technicians who also made the trip.

Stan and Bob joined the second Messerschmitt conversion class. The other trainees included American Gideon Lichtman, who had flown P-51 Mustangs with the 3rd Air Commando Group in the Pacific, and RAF veterans Baron Wiseberg, Morris Mann, and Cyril Horowitz. At České, Stan and Bob found themselves thrust into an altered version of a European war they had never known. They flew German-designed planes with their metric gauges and wore the heavy coveralls (also German-made), goggles, and headgear of a cold-weather pilot. They also stayed in the same barracks and ate in the same mess hall as the locals. The two were photographed together in their fighter garb, two Jewish veterans of the Pacific War learning to fly Messerschmitts in the Czechoslovakian countryside.

At České, the group was initially impressed at the sight of the Me-109s. They knew the plane by reputation: a frontline fighter that was the equal of the Spitfire, the P-51 Mustang, the P-47 Thunderbolt, and whatever else the Allies had sent up against it. Certainly, when these men had volunteered none of them expected to fly a German plane but at least they'd be at the controls of a frontline fighter. The scuttlebutt in the mess hall about the dangerous handling characteristics of the Czech version, however, quickly dispelled them of that notion.

Training proceeded at a dizzying pace, not at all like the methodical approach of the U.S. Army Air Corps. Stan and Bob found themselves first in the Arado, a German-designed, two-seat trainer that reminded them of the AT-6 that they had learned on in the States. After two short check flights, they were cleared to fly with an instructor in an improvised, two-seat version of the Me-109. After logging less than an hour of airtime in that, it was time to solo.

Solo flights on the Me-109 were rudimentary affairs. Pilots took off, flew several short circuits around the base, and then returned. There was no formation flying and, more troubling for those who had not previously trained as fighter pilots, no gunnery practice. Nevertheless, by early June, Stan's and Bob's training was complete, each receiving high marks from their Czech trainers. Having spent fewer than two hours in the Me-109, the Americans were certified to fly it in combat.

Life behind the Iron Curtain was decidedly different than what the volunteers had experienced on their trek through Western Europe. There was little to buy in town and no night-life to speak of. During the short time at České, there was not much to do but train and shoot the breeze with the other course members and the Czech pilots. Once the course was over, Stan and Bob got a brief glimpse of a different Czecho-slovakia. On June 5, they drove to the Sudeten town of Žatec, where Schwimmer's fleet was already fully operational. They stayed at the Zlatý Lev, one of two local hotels, that had a lively bar packed with local girls and, it was later discovered, American and British agents spying on the Israeli operation.

For one night, the freshly-minted fighter pilots enjoyed some spirited fun in a place the transport crews had renamed the "Sloppy Love."

At 9 a.m. on the morning of June 6, Stan and Bob climbed into the rear of a C-46 for a three-and-a-half-hour flight over the Alps to the mountainous French island of Corsica. They were crammed in with a cargo that included thirty heavy machine guns, a propeller, and repair tools. They arrived at Ajaccio, on Corsica's west coast, at midday, where they received their first glimpse of the Mediterranean. A tight turn and steep approach placed them in line for the field's single runway. As prearranged with the head of the field, the pilot followed a jeep to a remote portion of the airport, so as not to draw unwanted attention. While it was refueled, Stan, Bob, and the C-46 crew had a leisurely lunch on a veranda, where they enjoyed a spectacular view of a sea so clear that they had been able to see its depths as they had passed over it moments before. After ninety pleasant minutes at the Ajaccio field, they were all back in the transport plane for the ten-hour flight that would take them the rest of the way to Israel.

The Ekron base where the C-46 was headed remained vulnerable to Egyptian air raids, making it unsafe to leave the transport planes on the ground during daylight hours. That meant landing around midnight, quickly unloading the precious cargo, and departing back to Ajaccio before dawn. The nighttime landings were tricky. Because Israel maintained a strict blackout of the area, no runway lights could be lit until the C-46 was within range. And because the transport pilots were learning the terrain, there was a good chance of over-shooting Tel Aviv entirely, ending up over Gaza in Egyptian territory. A few days after independence, two crews ferrying small transport craft from Italy had done just that, landing in Gaza and immediately becoming prisoners of the Egyptians.

This night, though, all went according to plan. Under clear skies the C-46 banked east over Israel's Mediterranean coast, reaching Ekron only four minutes after crossing into Israeli airspace. The runway lights shined just long enough to guide a safe touchdown. After the plane taxied to a halt, it was met by excited volunteers, waiting to unload the weapons. As the cargo doors opened, the warm breeze that penetrated the plane's interior was a startling contrast to the cold Czech nights. The crowd surged forward, chattering in Hebrew, reaching up for ammo crates, and basking in the thrill of another successful supply mission. Stan and Bob stepped out into all of this, the two newest members of Israel's lone fighter squadron.

Chapter Fourteen

THE 101 SQUADRON

In a pursuit ship, you're a one-man army, not a taxi driver.
—*Air Force* (1943)

srael had been fighting a multiple-front war in the three weeks before Stan and Bob's arrival. The Syrians invaded from the northeast, sending their best infantry brigade into action in the Jordan Valley, along the Sea of Galilee. Slightly to the south, units of the Iraqi army crossed the Jordan River and attacked the Jewish settlement of Gesher. Lebanese forces struck in the north, in the area of eastern Galilee, looking to join up with the Syrians and Iraqis in a combined attack on the large coastal city of Haifa. For the most part, the Israeli forces had blocked these advances.

The situation was more tenuous along the other fronts. On Israel's eastern border, the Jordanian Legion had made impressive gains, quickly capturing the Etzion Bloc of Jewish settlements and seizing East Jerusalem, including the walled Old City, on May 28. In the south, a two-pronged Egyptian invasion force had captured much of the Negev and, by May 29, was within 20 miles of Tel Aviv. With the fate of the country's largest city hanging in the balance, the nascent air force had finally made its presence felt.

By then, four of the Czech Messerschmitts had been assembled, and the still-secret weapons were hidden in a hangar, awaiting their inaugural mission. The army's general command planned to send them on a surprise attack against the forward-most base of the Royal Egyptian Air Force (REAF), near the Gaza town of El-Arish. In April, the REAF had amassed a force there that included seventeen Spitfires, and planes from this base were bombing Tel Aviv with impunity. A May 18 raid on the city's Central Bus Station killed forty-two and injured more than a hundred, and something had to be done to stop the onslaught. Neutralizing the field at El-Arish would go a long way toward achieving the first responsibility of any country's air force—claiming control of its own airspace.

On the morning of May 29, however, the military decided to scrap the El-Arish raid in response to the Egyptian drive toward Tel Aviv. The Messerschmitts, it appeared, represented the city's last hope for salvation. Lou Lenart, a former marine pilot, led the flight of four. Two Israeli pilots with RAF experience, Ezer Weizman and Modi Alon, were also assigned to the mission. South African Eddie Cohen occupied the cockpit of the fourth plane as the Me-109s climbed into the sky above Ekron. Locating the five-hundred-vehicle column in the barren desert was not difficult and, following Lenart's lead, the

Messerschmitts made their strafing runs. The flyers recorded several hits and a number of Egyptian vehicles could be seen smoking as the planes roared past. But with guns on two of the planes jamming, the damage inflicted by the small Israeli force was minimal.

As the planes formed up for the return to base, it was soon apparent that Eddie Cohen was missing and that his plane must have gone down. The remaining three headed to Ekron, but the drama was not over yet. On landing, Modi Alon ground looped. While he walked away without injury, his plane was a total loss. In a single, apparently ineffective mission, the IAF had lost half of its complement of assembled fighters—planes that the Jews had gone to such far-flung efforts to purchase and smuggle into the country.

To Muhammad Naguib, the commander of the Egyptian forces driving on Tel Aviv, the raid made an entirely different impression. No one had warned him that the Israelis had fighter planes and he certainly had no idea that the mission had nearly crippled the squadron. Expecting more attacks, he ordered his troops to halt their advance and dig in. It was the closest the Egyptians would come to Tel Aviv. The May 29 mission, however unimpressive, demonstrated the impact a Jewish air force could have on the course of the war, even as it highlighted the limitations and unreliability of the Czech Messerschmitt.

Within days of landing at Ekron, Stan and Bob went through the formalities of joining the Israeli military, receiving army numbers that were a single digit apart. Assigned to the 101st, Israel's first fighter squadron (and its only one for the war's duration), Stan and Bob met the graduates of the first Messerschmitt course, who had arrived a couple of weeks before. These included Lenart, Weizman, and Alon—veterans of the May 29 raid—and also American Milton Rubenfeld. The other members of Stan and Bob's course, including American Giddy Lichtman and RAF veterans Baron, Mann, and Horowitz, landed in the next few days. The planes were not keeping pace, but the pilot ranks were starting to fill.

One pilot who was not there to greet Bob and Stan was Buzz Beurling, whom they had last seen in Rome. While the two Americans continued to Czechoslovakia, Beurling was assigned to fly a Norseman light transport craft from Rome to Israel. On the morning of May 20, Beurling arrived at the Urbe airfield, excited at the prospect of again being at the controls of a plane. He took the Norseman out for several loops around the field to test its readiness for the long flight. After a third pass, he touched down briefly, raced the engine as though he were again on Malta at the controls of a Spit, and leapt right back into the air. But then something went horribly wrong and people on the ground saw flames shooting from the exhaust. By the time the plane struck the runway, it was completely engulfed. Beurling never had a chance.

Even without Beurling, the apparent success of the May 29 mission gave the fighter pilots reason to swagger, wholly apart from the cockiness that many of the men already felt as members of the country's only fighter squadron. While the 101 Squadron had a number, the guys also wanted a logo—something that would loudly proclaim their identity to friend and foe alike. One night, a group that included Alon, Lichtman, Lenart, Stan, and Bob gathered to discuss the possibilities. Alon proposed a scorpion, the symbol of his RAF unit, but the others were looking for something bolder. As it was clear that Israel's main adversary was Egypt, someone suggested that an Angel of Death made sense, a symbol of God's Old Testament retribution against the sons of that land. Stan said he could put something together, and he and Bob went to work on it. [8]

They designed a red skull, adorned with the goggles and flowing silk scarf of a pilot, on a red background. The rest of the squadron approved, and it was soon stenciled on the nose of all of its planes. One squadron member commissioned red baseball caps with the logo on the front, and they quickly became a popular accessory to the flyers' wardrobe. To some Tel Aviv locals, the 101st was simply the "Red Squadron."

The military focus shifted to Jerusalem, where some one hundred thousand Jews were trying to hold out against a Jordanian siege of the western part of the city. Before the war, supply convoys bound for Jerusalem had to ascend a narrow, winding road that was threatened by a Jordanian-held fortress at Latrun as well as a series of other Arab positions on the high ground all the way to the city. Now, that meager lifeline had been cut. Food and water were strictly rationed and the time left to maintain a Jewish presence in the Holy City was running short. The loss of all of Jerusalem, Ben-Gurion feared, would be catastrophic for morale and could doom the entire war effort.

An American volunteer named David "Mickey" Marcus found himself thrust into Ben-Gurion's campaign to save Jerusalem. As Marcus's presence in the country indicated, Israel's

---

[8] In 1950, the Israeli Air Force added another fighter squadron, the 105th, nicknamed "The Scorpion Squadron."

attempt to level the playing field with the established Arab armies through the hiring of foreign soldiers extended beyond the air force. The Haganah had sought a high-ranking American Jewish officer to assist in the organization of the army, given the paucity of Israelis who had held senior positions during World War II. In 1947, Shlomo Shamir, a Palestinian Jew who had formerly served in the British Army, traveled to the U.S. to recruit such a man and had found Marcus. A West Point graduate and colonel in the American army, Marcus had commanded a ranger school in the Pacific and jumped into France on D-Day. To his frustration, though, he had spent much of the war in the army's civil affairs division, helping to plan postwar occupation governments in the Axis countries.

Marcus's main responsibility was to break the siege of Jerusalem. He believed the capture of the Jordanian fortress at Latrun was the most direct way of securing convoy access to the city's Jews. Though Marcus was convinced that Latrun could be taken, two prior failed attacks made it clear to him that the army should not exclusively rely only on the success of military efforts to break through to the Holy City. He advocated for the clandestine construction of a bypass road through the Jerusalem hills, which Israeli convoys could use to avoid Arab positions and resupply the city. It became known as the "Burma Road," after the seven-hundred-mile-long transport road from Burma to China, which had been hacked out of the jungle by two hundred thousand Chinese laborers in the late 1930s and used by the Allies as a supply route during World War II. With international pressure building for a ceasefire, time was running short. If Israel did not capture Latrun or complete the Burma Road before fighting halted, Jerusalem's western half was likely to be lost.

Work on the Burma Road proceeded mostly at night, in an area concealed from nearby Legion outposts. There, hundreds of laborers worked feverishly to turn a steep and narrow dirt track into a road that would be usable by vehicles. Meanwhile, a third Latrun assault began on the evening of June 9. Israeli forces briefly captured the high ground, only to be forced to withdraw by a determined counterattack. The operation was scheduled to resume the next night, and in an effort to improve the chances for success, the general command—which had previously rejected a plan to send the Messerschmitts as support—authorized air strikes against nearby Arab positions. The Israeli Air Force opted to send two planes, each carrying a pair of one-hundred-fifty-pound bombs, in separate sorties nearly a half hour apart. The first plane would be flown by Baron Wiseberg, now using the *nom de guerre* Dov Ben Zvi. Stan was assigned to the second Messerschmitt. The targets were two Arab towns, Sar'a and Ishwa, where Legion forces were thought to be concentrated.

With the objective only a few miles from the base at Ekron, this would be nothing like the marathon missions that Stan had flown in World War II. A red-faced volunteer from England in faded khaki shorts provided a detailed preflight briefing. He took Stan to the top of the control tower. From there, the target was clearly visible. Gazing through binoculars for a more detailed assessment, Stan realized that he would hardly be out of the base's traffic pattern before he would need to start his attack run.

He climbed down warily and walked to a waiting jeep, his head down as he studied a map of the target area. The briefer continued to talk earnestly about the mission's critical objective, noting both the number of men and tanks the Arabs had hidden in the area and the emotional lift the local Israeli soldiers would surely feel at their first sighting of a Jewish fighter plane. Stan, though, had his doubts. He had not flown a combat mission in three years, and this one would be over unfamiliar territory, with distances so tight that an errant bomb could easily hit friendly forces. Most troubling was that he would be at the controls of a plane in which he had only logged a grand total of an hour and five minutes of flying time.

He climbed out of the jeep and struggled into his chute, sweating profusely in the glaring sunlight. Mechanics crowded around the Me-109, giving it a last-minute check. A few of them helped strap Stan into the cockpit. He glanced at the instruments and started up the engine. As he described it later, it seemed to snort with rage, fueling a tail-lashing frenzy as the Messerschmitt headed down the runway. Kicking at the rudders, Stan fought to keep the plane under control, sighing with relief as it climbed into the air. The engine quieted as he adjusted his flaps and reduced power.

Looking down, Stan picked up the target right away, stealing a glance at the map just to make sure. Scanning the sky for enemy fighters and the ground for flak, he rolled into a turn to line up his attack. As he set the sight and flipped the gun and bomb controls to "on," he started his dive, dropping to one hundred feet over the town. Despite all of its failings, the plane was reassuringly stable in a dive. From Stan's point of view, that was the best characteristic a strafing aircraft could have.

With the plane responding to the controls, Stan's confidence returned. He lined up the gunsight on the town's center, shut one eye, gritted his teeth, and pressed the fire button. A long line of sputtering tracers streamed through the propeller. Recognizing that he was slightly off target, he lifted his thumb from the button, corrected his aim, and fired again. Windows shattered below as figures ran through the town, trying to escape the bullets that raked the main road. Suddenly, off to the left, Stan noticed tracer fire rising toward him in deceptively gentle arcs. He rolled into evasive action, kicking the rudders. Over the rooftops now, he leveled out just in time to aim at a warehouse that was presumed to store weapons. As the building passed under the nose of the Messerschmitt, Stan pressed the bomb button twice, releasing his one hundred fifty pounders. Then he kicked over in a sharp bank as machine-gun fire rose toward him again.

Stan cleared the town and began to pull up, looking back just in time to watch with satisfaction as the bombs exploded on target. With little time to revel in the accomplishment, he circled back for another strafing run. He completed three passes in all, paying particular attention to whatever vehicles he could find. With his ammo gone, Stan banked for the short return to Ekron.

Touching down, the Messerschmitt veered sharply, leaving the runway before grinding to a halt in the soft dirt just off the strip. The plane was a total loss, but Stan walked away without a scratch. Despite the rough landing, which he quickly shrugged off, he was in high spirits. He was debriefed about the attack and learned that spotters had reported good results from his strafing and bombing. Finally, he felt like a real fighter pilot.

Bob was anxious to get into the air as well. The next day, he was placed on alert, together with Israeli Modi Alon and Maurice Mann, an English volunteer. When two Egyptian Spitfires appeared over Ekron, Alon and Mann jumped into the only two available Messerschmitts to give chase. One of the Spits ran off immediately, but the pilots pursued the second in full view of their squadron-mates below. Once again, the Czech planes disappointed. Mann was in the position to get off a clean shot, but his guns jammed and the touchdown was another slapstick affair. Brake failure sent Mann off the runway and crashing into a Me-109 that Weisberg had previously wrecked. Alon at least was able to keep his plane on the strip, but he blew out a tire, and that grounded his Me-109 too. When one of the Spits returned moments later, there was no plane for Bob, and the pilots watched helplessly as the enemy Spit cruised leisurely back and forth over the base.

From the beginning, everyone in the 101st saw the irony of a Jewish air force relying on a Nazi fighter. As it became abundantly clear that those planes were less than reliable—astonishingly so—the use of German planes took on a different cast. As one pilot quipped: "The Germans must have known Jews were going to fly it someday." Stan also saw a kernel of humor in the incredible rate at which the squadron was devouring its meager supply of aircraft. After the chaos of the Alon and Mann flight over the base, he wrote a poem to commemorate the rapid demise of the squadron's fleet of planes, which he called "Ten Little Messerschmitts":

Ten little Messerschmitts, looking mighty grand
Ten little Messerschmitts, I.A.F. fighter command

Ten little Messerschmitts standing in a line
Gyppo flak got Eddie, and then there were nine

Nine little Messerschmitts still looking great
But Ruby had to bail out and then there were eight

Eight little Messerschmitts almost like heaven
The "46" just had to prang and we had only seven

Seven little Messerschmitts we're still not in a fix
So Ruby has to ground-loop and now there are six

Six little Messerschmitts quite stable in a dive
But Baron can't get off the ground leaving us with five

Five little Messerschmitts we're crying out for more
So Maury has to lose a brake and then they're four

Four little Messerschmitts the Gyppos shout with glee
For Stan forgot just how to land and now there were three

Three little Messerschmitts but we are far from done
But two are still packed in their crates meaning really one

One little Messerschmitt it all is really fun
Just one more operation and then there'll be none.

On June 11, just three days after Stan and Bob's nighttime arrival from Czechoslovakia and following a flurry of diplomatic activity, Israel and the Arabs agreed to a thirty-day truce. A few nights later, the members of the 101st were relaxing on wood and canvas cots in one of the hangars, still not sure if the truce would hold, when they were roused by a commotion outside. Several soldiers were attempting to load a wooden casket into a transport plane. The cargo door was high above the ground, and the soldiers were struggling to reach it. Stan, Bob, and two other Americans stepped forward to help. The addition of their effort was enough, and the plane took off a short while later.

The casket, they learned later, held the body of Mickey Marcus, the American colonel who had commanded Israeli forces in the Jerusalem area and who had only two weeks earlier earned the rank of *Aluf*, making him Israel's first general. He had overseen the successful completion of his Burma Road, traveling to Jerusalem on it himself and seeing with his own eyes the breaking of the Jordanian siege. He had only a couple of days to savor the triumph, however. Early in the morning of June 11, he walked away from his encampment to relieve himself. Upon returning, he failed to respond to a sentry's challenge—Marcus knew no Hebrew—and was shot, the last Israeli casualty before the ceasefire. The plane that left Ekron was taking Marcus's body on a journey that would end at West Point. There, under a tombstone engraved with the words "A Soldier for All Humanity," he would become the first graduate buried at the military academy who had died fighting under a foreign flag.

Though the ceasefire was set to last a month, many believed the fighting would not resume. Israel had halted the Egyptian advance on Tel Aviv, broken the siege of Jerusalem, and blocked Syrian, Lebanese, and Iraqi forces in the north. The Arabs had missed their opportunity to thwart the birth of the Jewish state. Continuing the war, it seemed, made little sense. For the men of the Red Squadron, though, it was hard to look on the bright side. They had come to Israel to fight and now it seemed that they had missed their opportunity. As he confided in a letter to Linden and Finley, Stan found the prospect of an abrupt end to the war disappointing: "If it's over I frankly don't know what the hell I'm going to do. I don't particularly relish the prospect of going back to some piddly-ass little job in L.A. or N.Y." The sudden halt in the hostilities also meant that his literary ambitions would remain unrealized: "If the war had lasted longer (by god, but it's inconsiderate of them) I'm sure I could have sold some articles. Now any such stuff will have lost its punch. So far as the book is concerned, I've collected some terrific material but it's background + preparatory stuff. The events which would have provided the rest of the story have been nipped in the well-known bud."

Chapter Fifteen

THE TRUCE

The Jewish people are not the derelict objects of charity. They are a proud people. They ask that they live in peace and dignity as a nation among nations, and be permitted to take their place in the world as a member of the family of nations. I raise my voice in salute to the new Jewish state—Eretz Yisroel. I raise my voice in praise of its heroic defenders. I raise my voice and call out that our own administration recognize this new state and raise the embargo against supplying it with arms.
—Congressman Leo Isacson, speech on the floor of the House of Representatives (May 14, 1948)

The U.N. appointed Count Folke Bernadotte, a Swedish diplomat, to supervise the truce and seek a negotiated end to the war. To assist him in his work, Bernadotte received a staff of truce observers drawn from the ranks of the armed forces of the United States, Sweden, France, and Belgium. One of his first decisions was to position nearly all of the truce observers in Israel rather than in the Arab nations. Though the truce prohibited both sides from bringing in men of military age, Bernadotte concluded that this provision would only be enforced against Israel, arguing that the Arab nations were already "abundantly supplied with manpower." The positioning of most of his truce supervisors in Israel also meant that it would face most of the scrutiny with respect to the other major truce requirement—that there be no additional importation of weapons into the region.

The one-sided inspection regime rankled the Israelis. It seemed to them that Bernadotte, ignoring Israel's military successes of the previous three weeks, was concerned only with helping the Arabs realize their aspiration to nullify the Jewish state. His ideas for a settlement included the transfer of Jerusalem to Jordan and the assignment of the entire Negev desert to Egypt—all as part of a program that would force Israel into a two-state union with Jordan in which the Jews would not even be permitted to control their own immigration policy. To many Israelis, it appeared that Bernadotte was an agent of the country's former British masters who had worked for more than twenty-five years to limit Jewish national aspirations. It was a view that Bob shared: "It looks like the Count is in the pay of the British, judging from the proposals he has made," he wrote to his older brother Harry.

Despite their reservations about the mediator and his proposals, many in Israel's military establishment thought the fighting might be over and began to look to the future. The IAF asked Stan and some of the others to remain, if the truce held, to help organize the postwar air force. Though he did not consider himself a professional soldier, Stan wrote to Finley and Linden that "it might be an idea for a while—just to get some dough." But he was not going to decide until the truce had expired, and "we see whether there will be war or peace." Despite the temptation of the training offer, his thoughts had started to turn back to the U.S. and the resumption of his life there. For that, he would certainly need a fast new car, and he asked his friends to put down a deposit on a 1949 Chevrolet convertible.

The movement away from a war footing left the guys with more time to explore Israel and form some impressions of the new state and its people. Stan and Bob went out to the countryside with a friend from air force headquarters. They enjoyed the visit—particularly Bob, who thought the friend's two-year-old reminded him of his own nephew back home. "His son is so much like Larry that I could hardly keep my hands off of him," Bob wrote to his sister-in-law. "He's about the same size, runs around a lot, talks a lot, repeats everything he hears, and the fact that it all comes out in Hebrew instead of English makes very little difference."

Not everything about Israel was so appealing. Stan found Tel Aviv too much like America: parts of it reminded him of LA (an impression that Bob shared) and New York's Rockaways. He was also bothered by the fact that, except for the occasional air raid, the residents of Israel's largest city seemed oblivious to the war. Even worse, he discovered there were "the same chiselers, brown nosers, politics, chicken shit, red tape, chairborne, and black marketers that they have in any city and any army." In general, both Stan and Bob preferred the Israelis they met outside Tel Aviv, who they found "tough and solid."

Whether they were from the countryside or the big city, Israelis shared one surprising trait. "[V]ery few people here look Jewish," Stan reported to Linden and Finley with amusement.

Though the other American volunteers had expected to be met in Israel with open arms as saviors, Bob had braced himself for a hostile reception. Given the U.S. weapons embargo, he figured the locals would lump Americans in with the British and be angry with both. That was not the case, he was pleased to discover. Still, the Israelis had their prejudices. They saw most of the men from the U.S. as spoiled and demanding while deriding volunteers from Britain as "nudniks." Only the rugged South Africans were uniformly admired by the locals. These attitudes could make the Israelis ungenerous and at times rude toward volunteers from the West. Many had already felt the sting of some version of what was becoming a classic, ungracious, Israeli refrain: "Why did you come, who asked you to come, don't do us any favors, we don't need you, we can get along without you."

To be sure, the volunteers had their own complaints. Many resented having to take orders from less-qualified Israelis in senior military positions. Though he was well-liked, air force Chief of Staff Aharon Remez had only been a sergeant pilot in the RAF with little combat experience. Munya Mardor, who was in charge of the air transport squadron, had never been a military pilot at all. The volunteers, by contrast, were almost all officers with extensive wartime records. Broken commitments were another source of frustration. A good percentage of the Americans, in particular, had received generous promises with respect to salary and insurance benefits, and these were not being fulfilled.

Stan during his teenage years.
(Courtesy of Ellen Brener)

Stan (sitting, far right) at CCNY.
(Courtesy of Ellen Brener)

Stan's "Coming Events Cast Their Shadow" drawing in the CCNY Yearbook.

Stan during training in South Carolina.
(Courtesy of Ellen Brener)

Stan in his dress uniform, with his pilot's wings. (Courtesy of Esther Hoch)

Stan (top row, far right) with the Air Apaches. (Courtesy of Joel Newman)

One of the squadron's B-25's on an attack run against a Japanese ship. (Courtesy of Vincent Gadbois)

Self-portrait during the war years.
(Courtesy of Esther Hoch)

One of Stan's pencil sketches during his
time at San Marcelino.
(Courtesy of Joel Newman)

Stan after returning from the Pacific.
(Courtesy of Ellen Brener)

Examples of Stan's art.
(Courtesy of Esther Hoch)

Stan after returning from the Pacific.
(Courtesy of Ellen Brener)

Bob Vickman
(Israel Military Archives)

One of Bob's drawings.

Virginia (top left) in her WAVE uniform during the war. (Courtesy of Jennifer Webb)

Marilyn Buferd, Miss America 1946, after winning the Miss California contest (mptvimages.com).

Stan's oil portrait of Virginia. (Courtesy of Jennifer Webb)

Stan and Bob at Zatec.
(Courtesy of Paul Reubens)

George "Buzz" Beurling.
(Matteo Omied / Alamy Stock Photo)

Vickman and Beurling in Rome.
(Israel Military Archives)

Beurling's plane in flames.
(Israel Military Archives)

...an (third from left) relaxing with other members of the 101 Squadron, including Bob Vickman (far right) and Lou Lenart (third from right). (Courtesy of Paul Reubens.)

101 Squadron logo.

Stan socializing in Israel.
(Courtesy of Ellen Brener)

Stan next to an Me-109.
(Israel Military Archives)

Stan with Congressman Leo Isaacson.
(Courtesy of Ellen Brener)

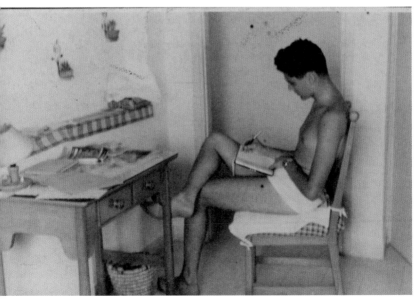

Stan writing in Israel.
(Courtesy of Ellen Brener)

Egyptian soldiers with part of the wreckage of Bob's Me-109.
(Israel Military Archives)

Stan as Major Stanek.
(Courtesy of Red Finkel)

Stan and Colonel Baruch.
(Courtesy of Ellen Brener)

A newspaper headline, after the successful smuggling of the Beaufighters.

David Judah.
(Israel Military Archives)

Len Fitchett.
(Courtesy of Roy Fitchett)

The Tegart Fortress at Iraq Suedan – The Monster on the Hill.
(Israel Military Archives)

The downed Beau on fire.
(Israel Military Archives)

The Beaufighter wreckage.
(Israel Military Archives)

The portrait of Stan on Is's wall.
(Courtesy of Ellen Brener)

An Israeli F-16 with the 101 logo.
(Amos Dor / Alamy Stock Photo)

Bob did not share the complaints of other volunteers about money. Instead, ever the hard worker, he was exasperated by the disorganization that he saw all around him. It seemed to him that too many Israelis liked doing things the hard way. He had "come near to blowing [his] stack on several occasions," he wrote to his brother Harry and wondered if it was different at the front where efficiency would presumably be more valued.

Stan and Bob were staying at the Yarkon Hotel, just a block from the beach, and Bob went for a swim every afternoon, a habit he had developed during his World War II service in the Pacific. They had menial air force jobs to occupy a small part of the daylight hours, which did not prevent them from finding time to start planning a possible movie based on their experiences in Israel. As always, Stan had no problem keeping his nights busy. He was now running around with a dancer, and Bob, who thought the local girls were trouble, could only look on with amusement. He dubbed his friend "Mink," in recognition of Stan's prolific night work.

Stan was not the only member of the squadron who enjoyed a rich nightlife. The pilots and other members of the IAF who were housed in Tel Aviv's hotels had developed a number of favorite watering holes. There was the Atom Bar, where a flyer could have a drink with other soldiers, enjoying the camaraderie of other men involved in the fighting. But for female company, the Park Hotel, with its bustling bar and dance floor, was the chosen destination. As the elite of the country's new air force, the fighter pilots of the 101st found themselves to be extremely popular among the women at the Park.

A pilot's wings, however, were not always enough to entice the ladies. A sidearm, some of the men felt, made an even greater impression, and there was hearty competition over the squadron's meager supply of revolvers. Stan was scornful of the practice, which he associated with "wheels" who had no combat reason to carry a gun, and a poem seemed to him as good a way as any to express his feelings:

> I tell you boys it's tough to be a wheel
> It's tough to have a gun you gotta steal
> It's quite a fright
> Might have to fight
> For the dangers at the Yarkon make your
> blood congeal.
>
> I guess I've had a million guns or more
> From .25's to great big .44's
> But now I've found the gun
> The one, the only one
> Hey wheel, watcha gonna do?
>
> I'm gonna buy a .38 that I can call my own
> Then I'll really be a 'schwitzer' tried and true
> With their dirty, unpressed clothes
> Will have to wear a lousy .22
>
> When I go out on dates
> I'll have it with me
> I'll be the sharpest 'schwitz' you ever saw
> Those flying chumps can get their lumps and
> ask for more
> I'll fly my missions on the Park dance floor.

On the evening of Monday, June 21, Bob received orders to meet the following day with some of the army's radio specialists as part of a broader effort to try to improve air-to-ground communication. The next morning, as Bob prepared to leave for his assignment, a pilot named Junior Pechner drove up to the hotel and reported that there was fighting in the streets near the waterfront. The others thought he was crazy, but when Pechner remained adamant, Stan and Bob went to investigate.

As they got closer to the water, they definitely could hear shooting. Bystanders told them that the *Irgun Zvai Leumi*, the underground Jewish fighting force that had once battled the British and was now fighting independently in Jerusalem, was trying to beach a landing craft that was loaded with weapons, in clear violation of the truce. The ship had hit a sandbar and it was stuck a few hundred yards offshore. When regular army troops opened fire on the ship, named the *Altalena*, the Irgunists on board shot back. The streets of Tel Aviv cleared, with people racing into buildings to avoid a stray bullet.

Stan and Bob ran back to the Yarkon for the movie camera. From the hotel roof, Bob shot some footage of the ship which, having sustained a direct hit, was now in flames. With smoke beginning to cloud their view, the two descended from their vantage point and made their way back to the beach. Irgun fighters controlled the area, and the Americans were repeatedly asked to identify themselves. Each time, explaining that they were pilots was enough to obtain passage. Several of the Irgunists even cautioned the pair to be careful, telling them that there were too few pilots in the country already. The Irgun fighters' concern for soldiers not from their ranks affected both Stan and Bob deeply.

The confrontation with the Irgun ship had actually started the day before when some of the weapons it was delivering were unloaded near a kibbutz called Kfar Vitkin. The Irgun had always intended to turn most of the weapons over to the army, but it wanted to keep 20 percent for its Jerusalem units, which were not yet integrated into the Israel Defense Forces. The demand caused the government to fear that the Irgun was building an independent army that one day could be turned against the IDF. Tensions rose at Kfar Vitkin before the *Altalena* pushed back out to sea and headed toward Tel Aviv. Irgun leaders were confident that Ben-Gurion would not approve an attack on the ship in full view of both the city's residents and the foreign correspondents based there.

The general command dispatched several navy ships and raised with the IAF the idea of bombing the *Altalena* from the air. In the end, the naval and ground forces sufficed, with the ship's fate sealed by an artillery shell fired from shore that set the cargo on fire and claimed the lives of fourteen crewmembers. The episode left a bitter taste in the mouths of the volunteers. Already angry over broken promises and the unprofessionalism of the IAF, most were furious that any thought had been given to sending an air force plane against a Jewish ship, and they wanted to make sure there would be no future attempt to use the IAF against domestic opponents. At a contentious meeting four days later, Hyman Shamir, the air force's deputy chief of staff, met with the pilots to ease the tension.

Stan's self-identification as a Jew had grown steadily since his time in the American army. Gone now was any ambivalence he had earlier felt. He approached the debate over the *Altalena* as if it were a question of identity. Speaking for many at the meeting, he told Shamir: "Without us, those airplanes can't be flown. And nobody can make us fly them. I for one refuse to participate in a civil war, and I refuse to lift a finger against other Jews." Correctly gauging the depth of hostility in the room, Shamir assured the men that no further thought would be given to using the air force for anything other than normal combat operations.

A few days later, Leo Isacson arrived in Israel, the first American congressman to pay a visit to the Jewish state. Isacson was a vocal opponent of the Truman administration's Palestine policy, and that position had spurred him to a surprise victory at the polls. His primary focus of attack was the U.S.-led arms embargo and its disproportionate impact on the Jews, given the prevailing assumption that the British government continued to sell weapons to both Egypt and Jordan, with whom it had strong treaty relationships.[9] Stan and Bob sought out the upstart politician and they ended up getting together several times. Much of their conversation focused on the embargo, which Isacson believed violated U.S. law. The three men also discussed what the future held for the citizenship of those who joined Israel's military. Stan, Bob, and the other U.S. volunteers worried that service in a foreign army would be viewed as a transfer of loyalty that was grounds for the loss

---

[9] The Jordanian army was led by a seconded British officer named John Bagot Glubb, whose countrymen formed much of the officer ranks. In Egypt, Britain maintained a number of bases along the Suez Canal.

of their American passports. Isacson promised to address the issue once he returned to Washington.

With the ceasefire holding, Bob's desire to get into the air intensified. For him, the need to fly was not just about the thrill of combat. Weeks had now passed since the whirlwind conversion course in Czechoslovakia and he had been rusty even then. He felt a loss of confidence the longer he spent on the ground and knew that he had to go back up to again feel sure about himself as a pilot. The ongoing problems with the Messerschmitts, however, made training flights impossible.

On July 1, with the truce set to expire in just over a week, Bob visited the Atom Bar. Empty when he sat down, it soon filled with servicemen. A group of twelve Greek and Polish Jews—former partisans who were now in the infantry—caught his eye. One with a guitar sang a selection of songs in a variety of languages. For the Russian tunes, he was able to make his guitar sound like a mandolin. On others, he was his own percussionist, slapping his palm against the instrument's body. When he learned that Bob was an American, he played "Rancho Grande" in his honor.

As Bob enjoyed the show, he thought about how much he would like to be a part of this close-knit group of fighters. These men, he was sure, cared nothing about money, rank, or insignias, yet they were carrying much of the load in the war. He could not help but contrast their attitude with the complaining and infighting he had encountered in the IAF since the start of the truce.

As the first week of July ended, it became increasingly likely that the truce would not hold. Bernadotte's mediation was going nowhere, the Arabs were as bellicose as ever, and the Israelis were also not anxious to see the status quo preserved. While Jerusalem was being supplied by the Burma Road, Israeli communities in the Negev desert were almost entirely cut off, and the loss of that region to Egypt loomed as a real possibility. Bob expressed a common skepticism when he wrote to his brother that "the Jews have gained not one single damm thing thru negotiation in any time in history, least of all now. The only way that this country will ever get a fair deal is to get it the hard way."

With the war poised to resume, he confided that "I'm glad I'm in fighters." Even as he wrote it, though, he worried that such a pronouncement made him sound like some kind of militarist. He was, of course, nothing of the sort. As he told Harry: "[W]hen this is over, I'm looking forward to settling down, for a while at least, & do something of a peaceful nature—what, I haven't decided."

Chapter Sixteen

EL-ARISH

How soon and how decisively we win the war will depend on how soon and how completely we face the fact that today air power must be the backbone of any successful strategy.
—Alexander P. de Seversky, *Victory Through Air Power* (1942)

As the truce period drew to a close, Egypt remained Israel's most dangerous adversary. With the Royal Egyptian Air Force controlling the skies, the 101 Squadron could not stay at Ekron where its Messerschmitts were well within the range of the enemy's Spitfires and Dakotas. The field had already been hit several times and more raids were certain to come. Ordinary landings and takeoffs were consistently putting Me-109s out of commission even without the help of the Arabs, and there was no need to expose the planes to the additional risk of being destroyed by the enemy while still on the ground.

The IAF relocated the 101st to a small field near the town of Herzliya, one that was not likely to appear on the REAF's list of Israeli airfields. From the air, the single dirt runway could easily be mistaken for a road or a section of undeveloped land. Air traffic control was housed in a water tower, and there were no revetments or hangars to catch a reconnaissance pilot's attention. Instead, the planes were well hidden in groves that neighbored the strip.

The IAF hoped that the dirt runway would provide benefits in addition to concealment from the Egyptians. In Czechoslovakia, the Me-109 was flown off of a grass field. While the plane had been challenging to fly even there, things had been far worse at Ekron with its concrete runway. Perhaps, the thinking went, a return to a softer airstrip would eliminate or at least reduce accidents on takeoff and landing.

The move to Herzliya severely curtailed the pilots' active social lives. They were now a thirty-minute drive from the city's nightspots. Their new sleeping quarters, the Falk Pension, was a modest, one-story building with an internal courtyard that was just a short distance from the Herzliya field. Stan and Bob took up residence there in early July.

Though the squadron had moved, its top priority was unchanged: protect Tel Aviv from the REAF. Planning during the truce focused on the Egyptian air base at El-Arish. This was Egypt's most forward base and the location of the Spitfire squadron whose planes had largely controlled the skies over Israel during the first round of fighting. The first Messerschmitt mission on May 29 had originally been planned for El-Arish, but the flight of four had been rerouted at the last moment. The 101st wanted another opportunity to try to neutralize Egypt's Spitfires on the ground.

The IAF's attack plans assumed an orderly expiration of the truce on July 9. But as it became clear to Bernadotte, the U.N. mediator, that he was not going to be able to extend the peace, he panicked. On July 8, without warning, he evacuated his truce supervisors from their observation posts. The Egyptians moved quickly to take advantage of the void, seizing Hill 113—from where they could threaten Israel's largest desert settlement, Negba—and also capturing two strategically important villages.

The El-Arish raid had been set for dusk on July 9, but the sudden turn of events forced a change in the schedule, and the men selected to participate were hastily summoned for a briefing in a tent at the Herzliya field. All the squadron's pilots had been anxious to go. Everyone wanted to see action, but it had been frustratingly difficult to find. The math just didn't work. It was not just that the 101 had far more flyers than aircraft. The surprisingly poor performance of the Me-109 only made things worse, since every time a Czech fighter went into the air might well be its last, further increasing the pilot-to-plane ratio.

The squadron tapped Lou Lenart, a veteran of the historic first mission on May 29, to lead the four-plane attack. American Bill Pomerantz would fly as his wingman. The irony of flying a Messerschmitt was particularly acute for Pomerantz. As a member of the U.S. Army Air Corps' 325th Fighter Group, he had frequently encountered the Me-109 while flying bomber escort missions over Europe and, on a single mission, had shot down a pair of them. Bob was pleased to learn that he and Stan would fill the other two spots, with Stan to fly lead in their two-plane element. After more than a month in Israel, Bob was finally getting his chance.

On the night of July 8, Lenart briefed the group on the target and plan of attack that the four would follow. They would strafe the field at low altitude, looking to hit parked aircraft, fuel dumps, and any service buildings.

The flyers rose early the next morning. By 5:30, after a quick breakfast, all were in their cockpits. Lenart took off first, racing down the dirt field and rising safely into the air, no small feat for the Me-109. Pomerantz followed, and then it was Stan's turn.

Stan headed his Me-109 down the runway, right on the tail of the second plane. Almost immediately, he found himself blinded by a dust cloud kicked up by the preceding aircraft. Unable to see the strip, he veered to the right. One of his wheels lodged in the soft ground off the runway. In an instant, the plane was on its back with Stan unconscious inside, still strapped into his seat.

Bob shut off his engine and waited while a group of flyers ran to the overturned plane. As they pulled Stan from the cockpit, he began to regain consciousness. Still groggy, he was only dimly aware of what had just happened. Lenart and Pomerantz circled overhead, burning precious fuel as the minutes ticked by. Finally, Bob received the sign to taxi and restarted his Messerschmitt. He rose into the air without incident, then formed up with Lenart and Pomerantz for the trip south.

Within twenty minutes, the three were over the Gaza Strip, which should have put them within range of the El-Arish base. Dense cloud cover refused to clear, however, and Lenart could not locate the field. They searched for as long as they could, but with fuel running low, Lenart concluded that the mission needed to be aborted. He turned his plane around and the others followed.

As they flew back north, they came within range of Gaza's port, which was visible through a break in the clouds. Lenart spied a few boats and decided that attacking them was preferable to returning to base fully armed. He strafed the vessels, with Pomerantz and Bob joining the attack. As he left the port area to continue toward Herzliya, Lenart checked the sky behind him. He saw Pomerantz, but Bob was gone.

The Messerschmitts did not have radios, so there was no way to contact Bob's plane. Upon returning to base, neither Lenart nor Pomerantz could offer any information about what happened to the third member of the mission. That night, news came from an unwelcome source. Radio Cairo announced the downing of a "Jewish plane of the Messerschmitt type." The pilot, the report claimed, was dead.

In the course of the morning, all of Stan's and Bob's plans had been dashed. Bob was missing and had likely been killed. Stan was still woozy from his own crash and now overwhelmed with the news about his friend. Over the next few days, Stan could do little more than sit in a chair at the Falk Pension, disconsolate over Bob's disappearance. To the other pilots, he talked obsessively about Bob and the kind of person he had been.

Within a few days, the air force discovered the likely cause for the loss of Bob's plane. The Me-109's armament included a pair of machine guns designed to shoot between the blades of the spinning propeller. A delicate synchronization mechanism permitted such firing. However, after several pilots returned to base with bullet holes in their props, it became clear that the synchronization mechanism was not working properly, yet another terrible flaw in the Czech Messerschmitt. When Bob had opened fire, he had likely shot off his own propeller.

Though others were skeptical that Bob had really been killed, Stan tended to believe the Radio Cairo report. He could not think of a logical reason why the Egyptians would claim that the Messerschmitt pilot was dead if it wasn't true. The doubts of others made him want to probe further, however, before fully resolving the question of Bob's fate. But after Stan became convinced there was no hope, and once the family had received official notification from the IAF about the disappearance, he knew that he could not put off any longer writing a letter to the Vickmans to express his sorrow.

That official notification to the Vickmans had been slow to arrive. A month after the mission, Bob's parents Mordecai and Elsie Vickman still had no idea that anything was amiss. Nevertheless, it had been some time since Bob, always a faithful correspondent, had last written, and they were becoming anxious. Mordecai wrote to his son on August 9, gently chiding him about the silence, explaining that everyone was "getting worried about you." He talked briefly about the family, before urging Bob to start writing again: "Perhaps you can now write a bit more than before, and [I] do hope you will write with good news."

Bob's disappearance placed a spotlight on the IAF's lack of preparedness for dealing with the special needs of foreign volunteers or, in this case, their families. It was not until later in August that Israel finally alerted the Vickmans that Bob was missing in action. Even then, that notice came in the form of a telegram, rather than an in-person visit by someone who might have been able to answer the questions that the shattering notification inevitably triggered. Elsie immediately sprang to action, contacting the American State Department and repeatedly pressing for more information about her son's whereabouts.

In Israel, Stan continued to mourn for his friend. He confided his feelings about Bob into a notebook: "I want to write about my friend; for he is dead. I do not want to write dramatically because he was not a dramatic person," he began. He wrote, he explained "[s]o that you may know why he was my friend and so, perhaps, that you may grieve with me, for he is dead." Stan felt a responsibility to strike the right tone: "I do not want to beat my chest or tear my hair or wave a flag, for he could do none of those things. And I do not want to make a pious mockery of a relationship of which I was very proud."

He thought of those aspects of Bob's personality that had been so compelling: "I never met anyone in the two years I'd known him who did not like him immediately—and I say this not because he was my friend + because he is dead, but because it is true. He spoke quietly, only rarely, but when he did, he did not lie, or boast, or try to make an impression. He said what he thought, sometimes awkwardly and often stiffly but always it was what he thought." And yet, Bob had a delightful sense of humor, often expressed in a "sharp, droll comment uttered in his solemn deadpan manner so that you had to look at him twice to make sure he wasn't serious."

The act of writing did not lessen the pain. His friendship with Bob had cost him deeply, and in a moment of self-pity,

Stan berated himself over it. He had violated, he thought, a cardinal rule of the combat soldier. "You should never make friends during a war," he told a fellow pilot during the darkest days following Bob's disappearance.

Chapter Seventeen

MAJOR ANDRE STANEK

He hates war and will go to any length to preserve the peace; but
[...] there is a point where you'd better stop imposing on a Jew.
—Lloyd C. Douglas, *The Robe* (1942)

Though Stan recovered from his physical injuries within a few days, he was officially off of flying status. That decision had been made by Dr. Louie Miller, recently appointed as the IAF's first chief psychologist. Miller, a South African, had an army background and had never before worked with airmen. However, since he spoke no Hebrew, he was disqualified from working with Israel's infantry, whose ranks included few Westerners. The air force was where the English speakers were.

Miller developed a policy of immediately grounding pilots who had been involved in an accident, and Stan had fallen victim to it. The air force did not yet have any formal mechanism for investigating whether a crash was caused by pilot error or mechanical failure and Miller did not concern himself with such issues. A pilot with a wrecked plane on his resume was grounded, and that was that.

Stan's grounding had little immediate consequence. By July 18, a second truce had taken effect, and the planes of the 101st were again idle. The portion of the war from July 9 to 18, which came to be known as the "Ten Days Fighting," had been largely productive for Israel. It consolidated its positions in the north, driving most of the irregular Arab forces from the Galilee region while blocking any further Syrian or Lebanese advance. The army also secured Jewish control over the western part of Jerusalem, and there was no longer a fear the Jordanians would succeed in capturing the entire city. And in the south, the danger of an Egyptian assault on Tel Aviv had been removed once and for all.

Not everything had gone Israel's way, however. Egypt's quick strike after the premature end of the first truce had strengthened its siege of the Negev. Now, Egypt controlled the high ground to the north of Israel's desert enclaves, cutting them off from supply or reinforcement by land. That control was centered around two hilltops known as Iraq Suweidan and Iraq el-Manshiya, where the Arabs occupied former British fortresses that had proven nearly impervious to Israeli ground attacks. If the fighting were to resume, there was no doubt that the action would be in the Negev.

Still, unlike the first truce, this one did not have a fixed end date, and a resumption of hostilities was not a certainty. After the Ten Days Fighting, many of the volunteers sought permission to return home. Some were convinced the war was over and felt that it was time for them to resume their civilian lives. Others had had enough—broken promises, inefficiency, and a general lack of appreciation had sapped them of their initial idealism. On August 2 alone, fifty of them met with a special commission set up by the air force to process petitions to leave the country.

The wave of requests created a potential disaster for the IAF. Nearly every one of its significant operational positions was filled by a non-Israeli. While the integration of the volunteers presented challenges, they also could not easily be replaced. There had not yet been enough time to train new Israeli recruits to fly frontline combat aircraft and there was no way to instantly replicate the foreigners' years of wartime training and experience. Greater efforts were therefore made to find new positions for disgruntled volunteers, as a way to keep them in the country and available to the IAF. While Ben-Gurion wanted to see an air force that was Israeli at its core with just a small number of foreign volunteers mixed in, that goal was clearly several years away.

It was now apparent to Stan that he did not have a future in the 101 Squadron. The grounding was only part of the problem. Even with the departure of some of the volunteers, there were still far more pilots than planes. The real issue was that the 101st had an abundance of men who had combat experience in fighters and thus had a far stronger claim to the cockpit of a Messerschmitt than a converted bomber pilot like Stan. Chris Magee, who had arrived on June 29, was one of these. As a member of VMF 214, Pappy Boyington's famed Black Sheep Squadron, Magee had recorded nine and a half kills against the Japanese in World War II, earning a Navy Cross. Rudy

Augarten was another new arrival with a distinguished fighter pilot's resume. At the controls of a P-47 Thunderbolt, Augarten had shot down two German Messerschmitts in a single dogfight, shortly after D-Day. If Stan were to stay, he was going to have to find something else to do.

The advent of the second truce meant the imminent return of the U.N.'s observers, and they would again be bent on uncovering evidence of Israeli arms smuggling. The IAF thought it vital to find an air force man to act as a liaison to those observers, someone who understood air issues and could defend Israel's position in meetings with officers from the U.S., French, Belgian, and Swedish Air Forces who made up the observer ranks. Lenart and others within the IAF thought that Stan might be well-suited for the post. They proposed his nomination to David Judah, a South African volunteer who was the IAF's chief of operations, and Judah agreed. Because the position would bring Stan into contact with truce supervisors who held senior officer ranks, the IAF believed that to be credible, their representative would also need to be a senior officer. It decided to give Stan the temporary rank of major and, on July 30th, Judah signed the order.

The presence of Americans among the U.N. observers presented a dilemma for Stan, rekindling fears about his citizenship. It was one thing to quietly serve on an Israeli air base, far from the prying eyes of the U.S. government. Having direct dealings with active members of the American military was decidedly riskier. Stan knew that his counterparts would immediately identify him as one of theirs, and it would then be child's play for them to probe for details about his background.

The distance from there to a postwar challenge to his citizenship would not be great.

When he and Bob had originally made their plans to come to Israel, they had intended to use false names. They had even picked out their new identities—Mark Dane (Stan) and Ken Magdrop (Bob). The use of those names had not seemed necessary when they first arrived in Israel and joined the 101st but as Stan prepared to begin his position as liaison to the U.N., the idea of using a *nom de guerre* now seemed like a sensible one. He chose Andre Stanek, a name that would allow friends to address him as "Stan," even in the presence of U.N. inspectors, without arousing suspicion. The IAF agreed to go along and, on August 1, the appointment of Stanley Andrews as liaison to the U.N. was canceled. The same day, Major Andre Stanek was appointed to the post.

Stan left the Falk Pension and returned to the Yarkon Hotel. He was back in Tel Aviv, where he could again take advantage of the thriving nightlife, this time adorned with a major's clusters. The army had its own liaison with the U.N.—Lieutenant Colonel Baruch Komarov, a Russian-born Israeli who had been a senior Haganah commander before the war. He and Stan would be working closely together, with Stan reporting to Judah and Komarov to Yigael Yadin, the army's chief of operations.[10] Given the diplomatic overtones of their work, Stan and Komarov would be assisted by Reuven Shiloah,[11] a senior representative of the foreign ministry.

---

[10]   After the war, Yadin would become the Israeli army's second chief of staff.
[11]   In 1949, Shiloah became the first head of Israel's spy agency, the Mossad.

With the transport flights from Czechoslovakia continuing, Israel's main priority was keeping the U.N. from discovering this clear violation of the arms embargo. That would be no easy task, as Count Bernadotte again decided that "the main work of observation" would occur in Israel, a decision that ensured continued Israeli distrust of his impartiality and disdain for the fairness of the entire inspection regime. Bernadotte stationed the Truce Supervision Headquarters in Haifa and most of his inspectors in Jewish territory. By August 1, ninety-three of the one hundred thirty-one observers were based in Israel, supported by eighteen planes and four ships.

Stan's biggest challenge was to deter U.N. observers from inspecting Ekron, where the transport planes landed, and Ramat David, where the IAF had gathered a heavy bomber squadron made up of three war-surplus B-17s that Israel had smuggled out of the U.S. just before the end of the Ten Days Fighting. There would be more than five hundred takeoffs and landings at Ekron during August, and that same month, an internal air force memo would identify Ramat David as the country's "most important" air base. Stan's ploy was to notify the U.N. that both bases were "secret research facilities" and therefore off-limits to inspectors. In an August 3 memo to the base commanders, he alerted them to the scheme: "You will not, under any circumstances whatsoever, clear any flights to these two stations. You will not volunteer any information on them. You will re-route all flights in their general area specifically not to pass over them. You will immediately contact me if any requests are made by U.N. Observers to fly to, or over these stations."

Stan made it clear to the base commanders of Ekron and Ramat David the aggressive steps they should take to prevent any attempted unauthorized landing at their fields. "Any attempt to land at your fields by U.N. planes will be met first by red fares, then trucks driven out on the runway, and finally, if they persist and land safely, armed guards to arrest and hold all passengers and crew in a secluded room, until I, or my representative can arrive."

On August 3, Stan first encountered Lieutenant Colonel Eric Gardin, the chief air observer for the U.N. forces stationed in the area. Gardin, a Swede, had been his country's air attaché to Nazi Germany during the Second World War.[12] Stan took an immediate dislike to Gardin, describing him in a memo the next day as "a vacuous, small-eyed, equine faced old gentleman with a smug and giggling stubbornness." Almost immediately, the two men found themselves in conflict, the flash point provided by Stan's insistence that Gardin would not be permitted to inspect Ramat David and Ekron. As Stan reported later: "I said that I was sorry, but that there were certain fields that no one, absolutely no one, was going to see, and that was all there was to it. How then, he asked, was he going to count our aircraft. He wasn't going to count our aircraft, I said. Oh yes, he was, he said. Oh no, he wasn't, I answered. He again quoted me some of the Count's rules and showed me the sheet of instructions. For instance, he said, if we see ten Spitfires suddenly, how are we going to know whether you've just gotten them, or always had them. He wasn't going to know, we assured him. That was our business. He reemphasized his right to know. I

---

[12] Sweden, like Switzerland, remained neutral during the war.

told him that we were a sovereign nation, and that no sovereign nation ever gave up to any organization, even the U.N. the right to inventory its military strength or find out secret military information relative to that nation's security."

Stan predicted Gardin would be a source of further trouble: "It looks like we are going to have to watch out for Gardin. He very obviously thinks that we are defying him and trying to outsmart him, and that therefore he will have to be cleverer than us. I think he had this opinion before he ever came here, either from a long-established anti-Semitism or a recently and intensively instilled dose...." Stan was fairly sure about what was going to happen next: "I'm afraid that we now will have to expect frequent trouble from him, either in the form of repeated, sometimes picayune protests to annoy us...or quick clever trips to try to ferret out information, rushing out to a field (or sneaking out rather) before we know about it, trying to talk or bull his way through to count planes or facilities before we can get there."

While Stan told Gardin directly that the Ramat David and Ekron fields were off-limits, as Major Stanek he was also able to engage in more delicate evasion of U.N. efforts to learn what was happening at those key bases. The day after the confrontation with Gardin, Stan encountered Commander Akerblom, a senior U.S. member of the U.N. observation team. Stan set the scene in a memo to headquarters the next day, beginning on a light-hearted note: "At about 2200, 4th August, 1948, I entered the dining room of the Kaete Dan in wistful search for some odd proteins and carbohydrates which, because of my superhuman determination, self-sacrificial nature, and absolutely unswerving devotion to duty, I had denied myself the entire day." Akerblom walked up to Stan's table and suggested the two have a drink. "We small-talked for a few minutes; then, and in what was probably his best man-to-man manner, he said, 'Look, you don't have to answer this if you don't want to'—I assured him I'd answer almost anything. 'Well,' he said, 'every morning at about four, I hear planes coming in to land at Tel Aviv airport. Can you tell me what they are?' 'Mind you,' he hastened to add, 'you don't have to tell me if you don't want to.'"

This was of course a reference to transport planes from Czechoslovakia, by way of Corsica, landing at Ekron with new weapons being brought into the country in violation of the truce. Not missing a beat, Stan responded: "I told him there was nothing to it. It was merely new pilots checking out at night flying on different planes, training and nothing more. He shrugged and nodded, as if that's what he expected to hear. Then he mentioned the article that appeared in the newspaper concerning supplies being flown in from Czechoslovakia. 'They called me up about it, all very excited,' he said. 'What's going on,' they wanted to know. 'Well,' I told them, 'there's nothing to it. I know the guy in charge down here, a personal friend of mine, Stanek. I'd know if there was anything going on.' I assured him solemnly that there wasn't, and wondered briefly when I had become his personal friend."

Stan had always been a student of people—in college, he had written an essay about the philosophical divide separating the abstract and realistic artists among his classmates. With the Air Apaches, there were the "old combat men" and the "new boys." He turned his gaze now at the various inspectors who crossed his path, filling his official reports with rich, descriptive, and often amusing prose about them. Cooper, an

American pilot, was "that rare person, a quiet Texan." Colonel Matthews, another American, was "a not untypical Air Force career man, determinedly and consciously tough, rank conscious [and] abrupt toward inferiors, but definitely possessing the universal Air Force idea that an airman, particularly a pilot, no matter what his nationality, character, or present job, is twice as good as any ground pounder." Colonel Momm, a U.S. Navy captain, "impressed me as a slow, reasonable man, not very well informed on the situation, but willing to learn and determined to be fair, a man to present facts and logic to, rather than emotion or rhetoric." Lieutenant Commander Huff was "a friendly navy pilot, fairly clever I think behind a farm boy exterior. He's worked for Naval Aviation and digs for information but apologetically."

Some of Stan's descriptions were cutting. Of one inspector named Longmans, Stan wrote that he was "a man distinguished only by an unfortunate moustache and an embarrassing eagerness to please Gardin in every way possible." An inspector named Guiborg came off as "a pleasant, wholly innocuous Frenchman, who doesn't have a clue about what's going on, since he is a Navy man."

The position, it quickly became apparent, was a perfect fit for Stan, catering as it did to so many of his strengths and passions. He spoke eloquently and forcefully, relishing arguments over air issues with senior officers among the U.N. observers whom he found to be condescending and arrogant. Yet the diplomatic nuances of it all were not lost on him and while forcefully advocating the justice of Israel's position, he did his part to ensure that the meetings proceeded in an amicable spirit. The report writing component of the position catered to one of his creative aspirations for the entire Israel experience, from the time that he and Bob first planned the whole thing. And there were, finally, those major's clusters. For all his disdain for wheels, Stan always liked the idea of achieving higher rank.

As Stan took his first steps as the IAF's air liaison, most of the weapon smuggling continued to originate from Czechoslovakia. Israeli operatives were continuing the search for military supplies in other countries as well, however. A complex smuggling scheme based in England of all places, and involving nearly a half dozen medium bombers, was about to bear fruit. Stan's path and that of the Bristol Beaufighter were about to cross for the first time.

Chapter Eighteen

BEAUFIGHTERS

Have you seen anything of a couple of Beaufighters?
—Victor Van Berckelaer, *Daily Mail* (1948)

While Otto Felix was working with his Czech contacts to arrange the purchase of Messerschmitts, Emanuel Tsor was busy in the western part of the continent. Tsor was a civilian pilot with no military experience of any kind, but he had nevertheless won Ben-Gurion's confidence early in the war. Tsor did this by managing to purchase several light planes in Britain, the most hostile of the European countries, at a time when other emissaries were unable to close deals in countries like France and Italy that were far more sympathetic to the Jewish cause.

In June 1948, Ben-Gurion asked Tsor to return to the country that the Israelis had nicknamed *"Eretz Ha Menuvalim"* (the Land of the Bastards). This time the Prime Minister was hoping that Tsor could find military-grade planes. Ben-Gurion was especially interested in Spitfires, the dependable World War II fighters, and Mosquitoes, fighter-bombers that the RAF had used for reconnaissance. When IAF Commander Aharon Remez found out about the mission, he asked that Tsor also be on the lookout for a third kind of plane: the Bristol Beaufighter.

A fighter-bomber, the Beaufighter was introduced into service in 1940. Patterned after the Bristol Beaufort torpedo bomber, early versions carried four twenty-millimeter cannons in the lower fuselage and six wing-mounted machine guns. They were also equipped with a primitive radar system that allowed them to become effective night fighters during the Battle of Britain.

Tsor did not think he could get his hands on Spitfires, which had only a military use, but he thought he may be able to pull off the purchase of Mosquitoes and Beaufighters. He went first to Paris, where he recruited Bill Towel, a British pilot who had helped him on a previous purchase mission. On June 24, now back in England, Towel found a lot of ten Beaufighters for sale and recommended that they be purchased using a dummy aviation company as cover.

Though ten Beaufighters had been available, Tsor decided to only take the best seven, since several of the planes were in extremely poor condition. The "best" planes were themselves in various states of disrepair, both from neglect and a stripping out of all military hardware prior to civilian sale, and one was soon abandoned because of rust. Extensive work was going to be needed before the remaining six would be ready to be used in combat.

Previous smuggling attempts had alerted the British authorities to the fact that Israeli agents were hunting for aircraft in England, and security had been tightened in response. Tsor needed a cover story. While mulling the problem with Towel in a café, they met a young actress from New Zealand. She had been hired to appear in a movie about the World War II exploits of New Zealand's pilots, but the project had fizzled because of a lack of funding. This was the idea Tsor had been looking for. He asked the actress if she was still interested in making the movie, and she didn't hesitate, going so far as to connect Tsor to the relevant individuals in Britain's movie industry. Soon, Tsor was staffing a movie company and cobbling together equipment and crew for *New Zealand's Pilots in Action.*

Tsor recruited another operative, Terry Fairnfield, to be the public face of the project. Fairnfield established the Air Pilot Film Company, which quickly took ownership of the six remaining Beaus. Towel, meanwhile, looked for pilots to fly the planes out of the country. Tsor was on a tight "production schedule." On July 16, he issued instructions to prepare for filming. A few days later, he notified Remez that the Beaus would be leaving England on the 22nd of July.

The crash on the 21st of another plane that Tsor was trying to smuggle, a Halifax, scuttled the plan, and it became clear that greater precautions were going to have to be instituted. In the meantime, repairs on the six planes were causing their own delays—in the end, only five would be flyable—and the weather was unseasonably bad. Coordinating, let alone expediting, "production" was becoming complicated.

On the 23rd, stories started to appear in the British press about the Halifax incident. If Scotland Yard drew a link between that plane and the Beaus, Tsor's plan would be doomed. Towel thought it was still possible to get the Beaufighters out if they moved fast. However, it was clear that once the planes left, the ensuing publicity would put an end to further Israeli smuggling operations in England.

The film company proceeded with its arrangements, receiving permission to fly the planes from their field in Oxford to Scotland, where, they claimed, the views more closely resembled New Zealand's. Once the planes were in the air, they would change course and head for Corsica for refueling. From there, it would be on to Yugoslavia for any needed repairs, and then to Israel.

A new cadre of volunteers practiced takeoffs and landings, ostensibly in preparation for filming. On July 31, one of the Beaus crashed on landing, killing the pilot and triggering a formal investigation that further increased the risk of discovery. Tsor's response was to accelerate the schedule further, setting the first day of filming for two days later.

On August 2, the four remaining Beaus prepared for takeoff as the cameras rolled, the forty-person film crew having no idea they were recording a smuggling operation. Towel arranged with the Oxford airport to wait three hours before notifying the field in Scotland that the planes had taken off. That would place their expected arrival after the field had closed, ensuring that the planes would not be reported missing until the following day. If all went well, the fleet would have twenty hours to make good their escape—enough time to make it all the way to Yugoslavia.

At 8:30, the planes climbed over Oxford and turned for Corsica. When they landed four hours later, Tsor was on hand to greet them. There were a few mishaps on landing—a minor engine fire on one plane and a problem with a tail wheel on a second—but nothing that couldn't be fixed in time for the next leg of the journey. At 6:00 the next morning, the Beaus were off again, with Tsor on board one of them. There were some mechanical problems on the second leg too, but soon they were again in working order. On August 4, the planes arrived at Ekron and the following day Tsor briefed the prime minister on the successful operation.

As Major Stanek, Stan had been busy throughout the last phases of the Beaufighter operation and in the days following the arrival of the smuggled planes at Ekron. As Stan had predicted earlier, Colonel Gardin remained determined to inspect the fields at Ekron and Ramat David and to do so with little or no advance notice to Israel. On August 6, Gardin arrived unannounced by jeep at Ramat David and attempted to inspect the base. He was refused entrance by Stan's old friend from the Czech conversion course, Dov Ben Zvi, now the Ramat David base commander. Gardin called Stan to complain, and they reenacted their exchange from the 3rd: "Gardin asked me if he could visit Ramat David this afternoon. I told him he could not. Again, he asked why not. I told him that… Ramat David was an experimental and research station and we would permit no traffic. 'That means I cannot go there this afternoon then,' he said cleverly. 'That's right, sir,' I said, 'You cannot.' He hung up."

Within a few days, Gardin was at it again, aware of reports of planes having been smuggled from Britain to Israel and determined to get to the bottom of it all. On August 10, he requested permission to conduct a series of inspection flights on one hour's notice and was refused. The Swede took off anyway and attempted to land first at Ekron and then at Ramat David. At both fields, as ordered by Stan, the base commanders prevented the U.N. plane from landing by firing flares and then driving all available automobiles onto the runway. Still undeterred, Gardin was in the air the next day, this time not bothering to request permission at all. By noon, he was in one of two U.N. Austers that snuck in over the hills near Ramat David, touching down on the base runway before anyone had noticed their approach. Gardin was immediately placed under arrest, together with his French pilot and the second plane's French crew.

Stan received word of the incident at his office in Tel Aviv. He and Colonel Komarov met to discuss the next steps at the Kaete Dan Hotel, then headed to a local airfield for the short flight to Haifa. They waited, as Stan later described, for "the noble Swede to cool his aristocratic heels" before entering the office where he was being held. The conversation went back and forth, Gardin angrily insisting on his right to go wherever he pleased and Stan and Komarov answering that the observer had no right to inspect Ramat David without Israeli permission.

As described by Stan the next day, the exchange took on an increasingly bizarre tone. After a long silence: "Gardin signified his intentions of putting four observers at Ramat David. He demanded quarters for them, good food, and a casino! I told him to put it in writing." That was followed by another discussion of Gardin's "rights." According to Stan: "[F]or possibly the tenth time he [Gardin] waved his copy of Bernadotte's instructions. I told him that it was not the Bible. He took out his monocle, peered closely at its sheets, possibl[y] to ascertain the veracity of my statement, and noted this down too. Then he said, casually, that he intended to put four observers here at Ramat David, two at Aqir, four at Tel Aviv, four in the Lydda, Ramle, Peta Tiqva area, and then, watching me closely to see how many feet I would jump he added, 'and four at the field north-east of Netanya where you have the ten Spitfires, I mean Messerschmitts.' Just put it all in writing, I told him." The meeting ended a short while later.

After returning to Tel Aviv, Stan contacted Colonel Matthews, an American and one of the senior truce observers, to request a meeting with General Åge Lundström, Bernadotte's chief of staff. Within days, Stan was in a room with Lundström, Gardin, and a number of other U.N. officials. Stan started off, saying that he wanted to talk about some "unfortunate incidents" that had taken place over the previous days.

Stan turned specifically to the particular provocation of trying to land at bases without permission. This was not, Stan explained "the function of an officer," even one of Gardin's rank and position. If Gardin disagreed with Stan's interpretation of the agreements or if he considered them contrary to Israel's obligations to the U.N., it was the colonel's duty to inform his superiors. If those superiors agreed with Gardin, they would be responsible for entering a protest to the U.N. The colonel should not, Stan emphasized, have taken matters into his own hands.

General Lundström tried to minimize the incidents, saying that they were merely misunderstandings and that he couldn't see why Stan took them so seriously. Stan insisted that Lundström hear the full story. Stan gave a more complete description of the prior day's encounter at Ramat David, explaining that Gardin's written clearance for that day's flight was for other parts of the country and expressly recited "not cleared to Ramat David." Starting to recognize the untenability of Gardin's position, Lundström assured Stan that such a thing would not happen again. When a frustrated Gardin tried to defend himself, Lundström "shushed him." According to Stan's report: "Lundstrom admitted ruefully now that Gardin had been wrong, and when that unhappy individual tried to explain himself, the General gave him a long and severe lecture in Swedish, the tone of which made the meaning all too clear, despite the difference in language." With that, Stan's triumph over Gardin was complete—and from that point forward key Israeli air bases would remain off-limits to U.N. observers. Stan looked over at the Swede, almost feeling sorry for him, "his long face even longer if that is possible, his arrogant 100% Aryan stance noticeably subdued, his monocle dangling limply in appropriate dejection."

Chapter Nineteen

LOST GLORY

He was a good man, though weak in certain attractive, human ways....
—John Hersey, *A Bell for Adano* (1944)

At the same time that Stan was successfully navigating sensitive inspection issues, finally gaining the upper hand in his battle with Gardin, he was also locked in an escalating struggle within the IAF to keep his position. Shortly after his appointment, he had been at the Tel Aviv airport to meet with General Lundström. After the general's plane landed, his U.N. pilot walked over to speak with Stan. The pilot explained that he needed a wireless frequency that he could call in case of an emergency. That made sense to Stan—it was, he thought, the minimum safety requirement due to any aircraft flying in any territory. "Have your radioman ask for it," he told the pilot.

A short while later, a member of the base staff told Stan that signals would not give out the frequency. Stan walked over to the operations shack, where he saw the U.N. radio operator standing in front of a desk, as air force personnel discussed the matter amongst themselves. The radio operator left and Stan called Yechezkel Davis, the commander of the signals branch of the IAF, to get to the bottom of the disagreement. An argument quickly developed. Davis was adamant that he would not release any frequencies. Stan tried to explain that he needed to have an emergency frequency that a plane could call if it were in trouble, but Davis simply repeated his refusal to release any IAF frequency. Annoyed, Stan replied that he didn't particularly want any of Davis's frequencies, just one that would allow a plane in trouble to contact Tel Aviv.

Someone in the room, overhearing Stan's side of the conversation, pointed to a sheet of paper on the desk that contained a list of frequencies. Stan asked whether the paper contained the frequencies that Davis had been referring to. Stan explained that he did not know one frequency from another, but a plane must have some frequency to call in case of trouble. He announced that someone in the room should provide the radioman with an emergency frequency.

About fifteen minutes later, on the field, Stan again saw the U.N. official, this time with a copy of the sheet of paper from the desk. "Did you receive the emergency frequency?" he asked. The radio operator stated that he had always had the international emergency frequency. That was news to Stan—he had not realized that there was such a thing. "You don't need these then," Stan replied, and took the paper and tore it up. It was the first time he had seen the paper up close, and he noticed that it contained three frequencies.

The whole episode infuriated Davis, who filed a complaint against Stan with the IAF the next day. Davis believed that it was Stan who had made the decision to hand over the sheet of paper and that he had done so knowing full well that the U.N. already had the ability to use an international frequency. Even more serious was Davis's charge that the sheet contained secret military frequencies. He claimed that Stan's action had interfered with radio communications within the IAF—including those to the transport planes flying in from Czechoslovakia. He requested that Stan be court-martialed for having provided secret information to the U.N.

Stan responded with a written statement that vigorously defended his actions: "I now understand that a great to-do has been made over this incident, at least concerning my part in it. Frankly I consider this nonsense. Let me give my reasons: Regardless of the state of peace or war in a territory, all aircraft must have an emergency frequency to call in case of trouble. This is common aviation courtesy and must be provided by any responsible national aviation control. It is true that I can definitely be blamed in one respect—I did not know that there was an international emergency frequency. But assuming my initial culpability and ignorance why did not Signals, who should know about these things, tell me? That was what I was asking, not top secret, cloak and dagger information—I repeat, a frequency that the plane could use in the case of an emergency. If it is supposed to be common knowledge that a radio-man should have such information, why, again, did not Signals tell me this, and immediately settle the situation. From the tenor of their conversation (and bolstered, I must add, by this subsequent asinine charge) I assume that their action was motivated by nothing more than infantile pique. Certainly, there was no way of knowing that these frequencies were secret, particularly since they had been lying in plain view on the desk while the UN radioman stood there. And, as a matter of fact, I might say that there are no such things as secret frequencies, certainly not with our radios, since it is extremely easy in a day or two of monitoring to discover any ordinary channels that we, or anyone else, might use."

Davis's complaint and Stan's statement were both forwarded to David Judah, IAF's chief of operations. Judah did not fit Stan's image of a rear echelon, chairborne wheel. A former B-26 navigator in the South African Air Force, Judah came to Israel to participate in combat missions. He had been a member of the crew for a May 31 bombing of Amman, a mission that had provoked Britain nearly to the point of invoking a defense treaty with Jordan and launching a retaliatory strike against Israel. He was also a participant in a July 18 raid on Damascus. Though he was recently appointed chief of operations, he had not allowed his responsibilities to keep him out of the air.

Judah felt that the American volunteers were undisciplined, based largely on his experience in Czechoslovakia, where he had gone to oversee final preparations of the three B-17 Flying Fortresses, newly smuggled from the U.S. The crews for the heavy bombers, mostly Americans, had been galvanized by the prospect of a surprise attack on Egyptian targets on their way to Israel. Judah thought the plan too risky, but the American pilots—two former New York firemen among them—were insistent, and in the end, each plane was assigned an Egyptian city to attack *en route* to their new base at Ramat David. True to form and despite his misgivings, Judah had participated as a crewman on one of the planes.

It was dangerous to be on his bad side. Judah was regarded as "tough and uncompromising," even by the South Africans. The tone of Stan's defense—the sarcasm, the criticisms of signals—did not sit well with the chief of operations, and when he and Stan met in person, the discussion grew acrimonious. The exchange deepened Judah's determination to replace Stan, and he notified Colonel Komarov of his intention.

To Judah's consternation, though, it soon became clear that the decision was not entirely his to make. From his point of view, the air force had appointed Stan, so it had full authority to relieve him. The army, however, saw the situation differently. Both Reuven Shiloah and Colonel Komarov rallied to Stan's defense, saying that based on his work, which they reported to be "honest, tactful and understanding," there was no one more qualified for the assignment. They told Judah that he would not be able to "find a better person" for the job and urged him to leave Stan in his position unless the IAF had "an even more important task for him." Komarov also accused Judah of allowing "personal considerations" to interfere with his decision, a veiled reference to the hostile exchange the operations chief had had with Stan.

On August 14, Yigael Yadin, the army's chief of operations, also threw his support behind Stan, pleading his case to Aharon Remez, the head of the IAF. Yadin's letter emphasized the importance of the position, particularly given the determination of the U.N. to supervise air force activities, and asserted that Stan's recent experiences made it impossible to replace him. Judah pushed back, formally notifying Komarov on August 15 that Stan had already been relieved. A few days later, Yadin wrote directly to Judah, asserting that the IAF did not have exclusive authority over Stan. Thus, the order to relieve him was "unlawful."

Two weeks later, Stan was still on the job, communicating by memo with Komarov, Yadin, and Shiloah about an encounter with Commander Akerblom, one of the American truce supervisors. Stan had learned that Akerblom was overheard suggesting that all of the non-Palestinians in-country were Communists, insinuating that Stan, in particular, was linked to independent presidential candidate Henry Wallace. Akerblom had previously been connected to the House Un-American Activities Committee and seemed bent on establishing some kind of connection between Israel and the Russians.

All of this was dangerous, Stan thought, and he was concerned that the political echelon in Israel would not be sensitive to the nature of the Red hysteria that had been on display in the U.S. at least as far back as the HUAC hearings: "I don't think I have been able to impress the full extent of the possible danger inherent in such activities. It is not enough to be able to say that we have no connection with Communists. The people in the Un-American Activities Committee care very little whether or not their charges are true. It is not enough to state that Akerblom is a military man and not competent to make political decisions. This Committee uses as its experts such people as actors, movie reviewers and booking agents. And it would be criminal folly to underestimate or smilingly dismiss the effect of a blast from this committee. Few people who have not been there to see for themselves can comprehend the extent of the hysteria prevalent in the States today...."

Stan was especially concerned about the possible political ramifications of a HUAC investigation into the existence of a link between Israel and the Communists: "At a time when Israel is applying for a desperately needed loan from the United States and when we are hoping even to have the Arms Embargo lifted, all that is needed is a charge from this Committee that Israel is infested with Communists and the whole thing could go up in smoke. Believe me, decisions in the States today are not made upon the merits of the case, but purely on the question of whether it is anti-Communist or not, particularly so in an election year, particularly so during the present crisis with Russia,[13] and particularly so when Jews are concerned. There have already been attempts in Congress to link Zionists with Communists, and far too many people in the States consider the words Jew and Red synonymous."

Stan's view that U.S. representatives in Israel might be attempting to establish an Israeli-Communism connection was entirely accurate. From the end of World War II until 1947, the U.S. Consul General in Jerusalem, the aptly named L. C. Pinkerton, had regularly reported to the secretary of state on "Communist Activity in Palestine." A secret March 1948 memo from the chief of naval intelligence about the smuggling of weapons to the Jews reported the rumor that one of the smugglers "is secretly working for a Communist group in

---

[13] This was a reference to the Soviet Union's blockade of the western zones of occupation of Berlin, which had begun on June 24, 1948, one of the first major crises of the Cold War.

Palestine which is plotting to publicize this shipment as an American shipment when it arrives in Palestine. Reportedly, the purpose of this plot is to discredit the United States with the Arab nations." Even a sympathetic editorial concerning Israeli-Russian relations in a fringe local newspaper was considered worthy of a direct cable to Secretary of State George Marshall. The British, who still had the Americans' ear on Palestinian issues, were strong proponents of the theory that the Jewish state would be run by Communists.

The night after dispatching the Akerblom memo, Stan ran into several of his old friends from the 101 Squadron in Tel Aviv. They were in a boisterous mood. When they saw Stan, resplendent in his major's clusters, they became even more raucous. As Stan described it in a lighthearted August 29 memo to the air force: "At about 2300, 28 August 1948, I left the Gat Rimmon with Major Simcha, heading for the Kaete Dan.[14] As we passed in front of the Pils,[15] we saw a number of individuals slightly under the influence of alcohol, stripped to the waist, and cavorting in great glee over the sidewalks and street. I recognized them to be pilots of the 101 Fighter Squadron, an organization of which I was a charter member and to whose strength I am still technically attached. They are in the habit of invading Tel Aviv about once a fortnight from their advanced base in order, I believe, to see the big city, imbibe some choice liquids, and, in general, have a good time

---

[14]   The Gat Rimmon was a seaside hotel used by a number of diplomats, including both the U.S. and Soviet ambassadors. Mickey Marcus had also stayed there. The Kaete Dan was a small pension on the Tel Aviv beach that was used by the army.

[15]   The Pils was a popular local café.

and release some tension. They were releasing a considerable amount of tension at the moment.

"I endeavored, with Simcha, to pass unnoticed, not because I have no affection for my erstwhile fellow pilots (my affection is boundless, unlimited, and of a clear, pure nature) but because I recognized that in their present state of joyful exuberance, their pleasure at meeting their old comrade might burst its bonds. At that instant the bonds were burst. I was seized by one of the pilots who, with loud and gleeful shouts of 'Here's Stan, our old buddy Stan,' bore me in uneasy grandeur to the others of the company. There they noticed that, for some peculiar reason I can't at the moment recall, I was wearing a shirt. This seemed to perturb them. It was far too warm an evening for an old friend of theirs to be burdened with a hot, sticky shirt. Thereupon, and with great dispatch, they relieved this intolerable situation. In approximately thirty seconds I found myself clad only in the pitiful fragments of an undershirt (plus, of course, trousers, shorts, shoes and socks).

"In the course of this forceful striptease, some of my disrobers discovered that my shirt bore a Major's shoulder insignia, and they were extremely distressed that a person of my free and spirited nature should be laden with the cares and responsibilities of rank. Forthwith, therefore, these burdensome badges were removed. Since, at the moment, I was being joyfully clasped by at least four pairs of loving arms, I was unable to do much about this highly disrespectful action. The last I saw of the grape leaves, they were being born aloft in simple, triumphant glee by the clutching hands of my tender friends. When, some forty minutes later, I was finally able to break away, they were nowhere to be found, and none of my demonstrative blood brothers had the faintest idea what had happened to them. I must, therefore, regard them as irretrievably lost.

"In view of the above circumstances, I most respectfully request that a new set of badges of rank be issued to me, for which I shall gladly pay, in penance for my association with a group of low characters who show such little respect for the grandeur and glory that is a Major's."

That glory did not last much longer. Soon after the loss of his clusters, Major Stanek's career came to an end, as Judah finally gained the upper hand in his battle with the army. Stan's first reaction to the harsh blow was to join the crowd of volunteers looking to head home. The dismissal from his post as liaison to the U.N. left him with little reason to remain in the country. But as galling as the loss of the liaison position had been, it was the loss of flying privileges that really ate at him. He could not accept being told by an army doctor that he was psychologically unfit to fly because of accidents in a disastrous plane that no one could control. Stan prepared a formal request for discharge, explaining that "Dr. Miller has pronounced me psychologically unfit at present for combat flying. Since the only reason I came here was to fly combat I feel that now that I can no longer do so I should be free to return." Stan could not keep a dose of bitterness out of the request. "Further, if I am so maladjusted mentally that I cannot fly I know that any ground job would only deepen such maladjustment since I have always been unhappy on the ground while others fly."

Chapter Twenty

HOPE

*There is indeed a fraternalism in war that is
hard for people at home to comprehend.*
—Ernie Pyle (1945)[16]

While the support of Yadin, Shiloah, and Komarov had
not been able to save Stan's job, at least it put to rest
all notions of a court-martial. The IAF would not seek
further punishment for the signals incident. Instead, he was
treated as another disgruntled but skilled volunteer whose
prior position had not worked out and who now needed reas-
signment to be kept from leaving Israel before the war was over.

Abandoning his briefly considered plan to leave, Stan
agreed to become the air force coordinating officer to the army's

---

[16] Quoted in *Ernie's War: The Best of Ernie Pyle's World War II Dispatches*
(David Nichols, Ed.) (1986).

southern command, on the front with Egypt, reporting for duty in September. The post was a reflection of the military's growing desire to improve communication between air and ground forces. Properly coordinated, air attacks could soften a target, making the infantry's job infinitely easier. Without coordination, the air force would be irrelevant to the ground troops or, worse, a potentially lethal source of friendly fire.

Stan was instructed to work directly with some of the army's senior commanders in the area, including a young officer named Yitzhak Rabin, the chief of operations in the south and later Israel's fifth prime minister. Stan's responsibilities, as outlined in a memo from Air Force Commander Remez, included guiding the communication between air and ground forces, assisting with target selection, determining a bomb line and acceptable forward-most positions for Israeli and Arab forces, and directing aircraft during joint operations. He was even given operational command over the region's lone IAF squadron, which flew mostly supply and reconnaissance missions.

As Stan's IAF career started to look promising again, his carefully erected wall of secrecy began to crumble. His sister Esther discovered the truth about his overseas adventure and wrote a letter chiding him for his ruse and encouraging him to come clean with their parents. Stan responded with the apology his older sister was entitled to while trying to explain why he had hidden the truth: "I'm very sorry to have deceived you but at all costs I did not want the folks to know what I was doing. I remembered how they worried and aged when I was in the Pacific." For another month he maintained the Switzerland story for Joseph and Rebecca, on one occasion calming their fears about the risk to him from a widely-reported Swiss epidemic. Finally, in September, with the truce holding, he told them where he was and what he was doing, minimizing the danger: "Now, of course, there's nothing to worry about since there's no fighting, and in my opinion, there won't be anymore—or if there is, very little."

In the south, Stan learned about the first two rounds of fighting with the Egyptians. When the war started, there were twenty-seven Jewish settlements in the Negev desert with a total population of about three thousand. These communities were lightly armed, and only five had more than thirty defenders. The meager forces were supplemented by two lightly armed battalions totaling eight hundred men.

When the first truce took effect on June 11, Israel had been able to resupply its Negev settlements by convoy traveling along the north-south road from Rehovot to the Negev. However, during what was supposed to have been a lull in the fighting, the Egyptians had seized a number of outposts near the junction of the Negev's north-south and east-west roads, allowing the Arabs to close the road to Israeli vehicles traveling south. Some settlements had to be provisioned by air, while the army could occasionally reach others with military trucks. The area controlled by Egypt, separating the Negev settlements in the south from the rest of the country, came to be known as the Isolation Belt.

During the Ten Days Fighting, Israel had not been able to break through the Isolation Belt to reestablish a reliable land route, so resupply was now entirely the province of the air force. Meanwhile, in spite of the second truce, skirmishes regularly flared between Israeli and Egyptian forces, each side looking to gain a tactical advantage for the next round of warfare. More than anything else, and despite his efforts to downplay the risk of more fighting to his family, Stan's time in the south left him with the growing realization that the war with Egypt was certain to resume.

In his prior post as liaison officer, Stan had talked to anyone he could about Bob Vickman's disappearance. In the back of his mind, Stan still held out some hope that Bob might have been captured alive and there was no telling who might be able to help in the search. He had been a one-man foreign service, reaching out to truce supervisors, the Red Cross (which, on his request, telegrammed three inquiries to their Egyptian counterparts who denied that they were holding Bob), and even the various newspaper correspondents he had met in Tel Aviv. He had pleaded his friend's case with the IAF and army during his time as liaison to the truce supervisors and now he continued the effort with his new counterparts. Still, through August, Stan saw no reason to change his belief that Bob had been killed on July 9. And then he heard a remarkable story that, for the first time, gave him hope.

Israel had captured an Egyptian captain on July 11. During interrogation, the officer revealed that the day before he had escorted several Jewish prisoners from army headquarters in Gaza to air force headquarters in El-Arish. One of the prisoners was a pilot. Stan was not aware of any other recently captured Israeli pilots. Further, it made sense that the Egyptians would transport a pilot prisoner to air force headquarters for questioning as soon as possible after capture. The information was clearly tantalizing.

To Stan's immense frustration, though, the Egyptian captain had managed to escape. Given Bob's unusual height and the fact that he was an American, further interrogation, guided by Stan, should have permitted an easy determination of whether the pilot could have been Bob. On September 15, he wrote to HQ Intelligence to make a formal request for the full report of the interrogation.

With that request, Stan also included information about another rumor that had come to his attention. This one was from Ezer Weizman, an old friend from the 101 Squadron.[17] Weizman had told Stan that during a trip to the Negev, he had heard from an army officer that informants in Gaza had reported on the existence of a Jewish pilot prisoner. The flyer was in good health, except for a backache. This was a common physical complaint of combat pilots who had crash-landed. Weizman's report provided additional evidence that Bob was alive and in Egyptian captivity.

A short while later, Stan received a copy of the interrogation report for the escaped Egyptian prisoner—a Captain Abba Hafez. The report was consistent with the rumors Stan had heard that the Jewish pilot prisoner that Hafez had escorted was in good health, except for a back injury. Stan now wrote a memo to Israel's liaison officer to the Red Cross, distilling all that he had learned and providing his own theories and suggestions: "It is very possible that Vickman is using another name—he is an American and might not want the American Consulate to hear of his presence in the Israel Air Force. He might be using the name of 'Ken Magdrop,' or anything else he might have thought up. I do not think, therefore, that it would

---

[17] Among his later positions, Weizman would become commander of the air force, defense minister, and Israel's seventh president.

be any use at all inquiring about him by name. They could simply deny having anyone of that name, as they have. The inquiries should be made according to his description, he was quite distinctive physically, his nationality, the date on which he was taken, the fact that he is a pilot, and the type of aircraft he flew. Any one of these points would serve to identify him."

Stan also provided a detailed physical description of his friend: "He is 25 years old, very tall (6'3"), very thin (about 165 pounds), has short, wavy, black hair, brown eyes, a broad, pug, uplifted nose, and a very bony, thin face, with particularly prominent cheek-bones. He speaks slowly and is usually very quiet." Stan supplemented his memo with a recent photograph of Bob, one that had been taken with Congressman Leo Isacson back in June. He closed with the following additional request: "Further, if the Egyptians claim he is dead, I think it is proper to demand proof, papers he carried, particulars of his name, location or photograph of his grave. These, or at least some of them, are obligatory, I believe, according to the Geneva Convention."

As he awaited a response from the liaison officer, Stan again pondered his place with the IAF. His new assignment was unsatisfying. With the war poised to resume, he wanted to fly, not coordinate the flying activities of others. He was also acutely aware that air-ground coordination was not truly his area of expertise. Of the more than forty combat missions that he flew during World War II, there was not a single one in which he had provided close air support for ground operations.

Two significant hurdles stood between Stan and a return to combat duty. Dr. Miller's grounding order remained in effect. There was also no longer room for him in the 101 Squadron, which was flusher than ever with experienced fighter pilots.

The more recent arrivals included John McElroy, a veteran Spitfire pilot from Canada who had become a double ace over Malta, and two of his countrymen, John Doyle and Dennis Wilson, who had also seen extensive action against the Germans and Italians.

Stan contrived a solution to both dilemmas. At the Ramat David airfield outside of Haifa, which was commanded by his friend Baron Wiseberg from the Czech conversion course, the 103 Squadron was taking shape. Its pilots flew medium bombers, mostly Dakotas that had been fitted with improvised bomb racks. In August, it had received an infusion of new planes, including the four Beaufighters that Emanuel Tsor had smuggled into the country near the beginning of Stan's tenure as IAF liaison officer.

More than any other plane in the IAF's arsenal, the Beau resembled the B-25 that Stan had flown as a member of the Air Apaches. While the RAF had deployed it as a night fighter over Europe, the plane was used extensively in the Asian theater for strafing missions against Japanese naval and ground targets. A number of them participated in the Battle of the Bismarck Sea where U.S. General Kenney had first proved the value of low-altitude attacks against enemy shipping. A transfer to the 103 Squadron might get Stan back into combat—and in a plane that was perfectly suited to his training and experience. He realized that now, whatever his original feelings about being routed to the B-25 rather than a fighter during WWII, he belonged in a bomber. If he was truly going to fight and to make a difference, his best hope for that lay in the kind of air combat that he knew as well or better than anyone else in the Israeli Air Force.

Chapter Twenty-One

OPERATION YOAV

Oh, I have slipped the surly bonds of Earth
And danced the skies on laughter-silvered wings;
Sunward I've climbed, and joined the tumbling mirth
Of sun-split clouds,—and done a hundred things
You have not dreamed of—wheeled and soared and swung
High in the sunlit silence. Hov'ring there,
I've chased the shouting wind along, and flung
My eager craft through footless halls of air...
Up, up the long, delirious burning blue
I've topped the wind-swept heights with easy grace
Where never lark, or even eagle, flew –
And, while with silent, lifting mind I've trod
The high untrespassed sanctity of space,
Put out my hand, and touched the face of God.
—John Magee, Jr., "High Flight" (1941)

Despite the small Jewish presence in the Negev at the outbreak of the war, David Ben-Gurion was determined to preserve Israel's claims to a region that was larger than all of the other land held by Israel in the summer of 1948. Control of the Negev would also give Israel access to the mineral resources of the Dead Sea and, potentially, a trade route to Asia through the Gulf of Aqaba. Without it, the prime minister feared that Israel would never be more than a "miniature state" with an uncertain future.

Ben-Gurion's focus on the Negev was not new. He had championed the expansion of the Jewish presence in the desert since the early 1940s when the British placed onerous restrictions on settlement there. Working against the Mandatory power, the local Bedouin population, and the sheer vastness of the area, he had presided over the establishment of more than twenty Jewish settlements and the laying of a pipeline system that kept most of them supplied with fresh water. Over the years, he formed what the U.S. State Department came to regard, with some derision, as a "mystical attachment" to the region.

From the start of hostilities, the Negev was the main battleground for Israeli and Egyptian ground forces. Some of the most heroic stands of the poorly equipped, numerically inferior Jewish forces had occurred in the southern settlements, at places like Yad Mordechai and Kfar Darom. Those communities were eventually overrun or abandoned, but a cluster of others remained in the northern Negev. These Jewish footholds were now in their own precarious state, with the Isolation Belt blocking the passage of Israeli supply convoys.

By September, the Negev was presenting Israel with significant military and political challenges. An IAF airlift of C-46 flights over Egyptian lines to a desert strip at Ruchama had replaced the worn-out Negev brigade with fresh troops and brought two thousand tons of supplies to the isolated Jewish communities, protecting them from collapse. The chief of staff was warning, however, that fuel supplies would not allow the airlift to continue for much longer. The result would be catastrophic if the fate of the Negev was not resolved soon.

The political situation was equally fraught. Count Bernadotte, the U.N. mediator, had wanted to give the entire Negev to Jordan as part of a peace settlement, unmoved by the fact that the northern Negev was within the areas assigned to the Jews in the 1947 Partition Resolution. The deciding factor for the Swede was the insignificant number of Jews living there—still fewer than five thousand. His solution was to "compensate" Israel by recognizing its war gains in the Galilee. Bernadotte's determination to cut off the Negev and his general favoring of the Arab position had continued to create enormous hostility among Israelis. Members of the Stern Gang, an underground group that had fought against British rule, acted in September. Three of its members intercepted Bernadotte's car at a checkpoint and shot him through an open window—killing him. One of Stan's former U.N. counterparts, General Åge Lundström, had been in the car with the count but escaped injury. The assassination had given Bernadotte a martyr's status and endowed his political recommendations with even greater force.

Everything was coming to a head as Stan joined the 103 Squadron. By late summer of 1948, Egyptian forces in the

Negev consisted of more than a dozen battalions, representing thirteen thousand men under arms, an increase of 35 percent over pre-truce levels. Israel had also made good use of the truce period. In addition to sneaking in the four Beaufighters, it had added several Spitfires and secured an agreement with the Czechs for the sale of dozens more. The fear that the invading Arabs might obliterate the Jewish state was now well in the past. For Israel, more significant than the question of how to defeat the strengthened Egyptian army was when to engage it. From the moment the second truce began on July 18 without a fixed end date, it was clear that war could resume at any moment. In the meantime, the need to remain on full mobilization created the very real possibility of an economic collapse.

Confident in his country's strengthened armed forces, Ben-Gurion argued to his cabinet that the hazards of a truce with no resolution were greater than those posed by a resumption of the fighting. In his estimation, the government now faced a decision as momentous as the one it had taken in May when independence was declared. To his mind, Israel did not yet truly have a state at all—not with invading armies standing on its borders or, in the case of Egypt, within them. Breaking through to the south was an essential step to achieving true independence.

On October 9, Israeli commanders received their orders for Operation Yoav, as the Negev campaign would be called. It comprised four phases. In the first, the army would eliminate enemy forces around the towns of Iraq Suweidan and Beit Govrin and capture Hill 113 and various other high-ground outposts in the north, breaking through the Isolation Belt. If successful, this would isolate the Egyptian forces and prevent them from mounting a coordinated counter-attack. In phase two, Israeli troops would capture strongholds at the towns of Fallujah and Iraq el-Manshiya. Opening the road to the Negev would occur in the third phase, to be followed, in phase four, by the interdiction of Egyptian supply lines between Gaza and El-Arish.

The IAF's Chief of Operations David Judah identified the air force's objectives for Yoav. First and foremost, it needed to disrupt Egyptian airpower, preventing further threats to Tel Aviv and protecting ground forces in the Negev from enemy air attacks. Judah also wanted to see an effective aerial bombardment of enemy strongpoints as well as the provision of direct air support for the ground troops. To help the air force achieve its goals, he insisted on close coordination with intelligence to ensure proper target identification and mission assessments. Toward that end, returning crews would be immediately debriefed, with copies of the reports going straight to operations.

Clearly, however, the neutralization of the Royal Egyptian Air Force was the highest priority. Accomplishing that task meant striking the El-Arish air base, where Egypt's 2 Squadron, with fourteen frontline fighters, was located. The REAF's forward-most airfield and launching pad for the strikes on Tel Aviv, El-Arish, had eluded the IAF's grasp since the start of the war. The first time had come on May 29, when the four newly-assembled Messerschmitts were diverted for a strafing run on the Egyptian armored column that was rumbling north toward Tel Aviv. The second had been at the start of the

Ten Days Fighting, on the Lenart-led mission where Bob had disappeared.

For this round of fighting, Israel had a substantially beefed-up air capacity and an attack on El-Arish would no longer need to solely rely on the unpredictable Me-109. In addition to the Czech fighters, now supplemented by four Spitfires and a P-51 Mustang, the air force could call on the 103rd's Beaufighters and Dakotas, the Hammers Squadron's three B-17s, a Skymaster and five C-46s of the Air Transport Command, five Norsemans that had been organized into a dive-bombing squadron headed by the son of a Baptist minister, and an assortment of light aircraft.

In his order of the day at the start of Yoav, IAF Commander Aharon Remez declared that the air force was being called upon to be the "tip of the spear" against the invading Egyptians and told his men that the "fate of the state and its people depend on us." By "tip of the spear," Remez was referring to the fact that the air force would lead off Yoav with the raid on El-Arish before the infantry would advance. This was an effort to employ the basic tactic of a successful modern army—neutralizing the enemy's air force before sending in the ground troops—something that had proven itself again and again during the Second World War. The effectiveness of the MacArthur-Kenney partnership had centered on precisely this, with the 5th Air Force bombing attacks paving the way for the dramatic American return to the Philippines in late 1944. Knowing the tactic was one thing, implementing it effectively was something else entirely, as the IAF knew only too well from the ill-fated July 9 raid where Bob had been lost.

Further complicating matters was the fact that, in contrast to the sustained aerial bombardments of the Second World War, the IAF would not have the luxury of weeks, or days, or even a single full day, before the ground offensive launched. Ben-Gurion was convinced that the U.N. would move quickly to stop the fighting, so the window for action was tight. He wanted to achieve all of Yoav's objectives in less than a week, leaving little time for a sustained air campaign.

It all began with a light Egyptian attack on an Israeli supply convoy on the night of October 15, which Ben-Gurion had expected and then seized upon as a justification for ending the truce. Within hours, three Spitfires had taken off from Herzliya, heading south toward El-Arish. By 5:30 a.m., they were over the target. Each plane carried a pair of thirty-kilo bombs, which they dropped from two thousand feet before starting strafing runs that claimed two Egyptian planes on the ground, a symbol of Egypt's failure to anticipate the raid.

Less than an hour later, two Beaus reached the Egyptian base. A Canadian volunteer named Len Fitchett flew the lead plane in his first IAF combat mission. The twenty-four-year-old Canadian had amassed a distinguished record with the Royal Canadian Air Force. He was overseas in May 1943 and saw service in two night-fighter squadrons. During the war, Fitchett had flown a variety of planes, including the Beaufighter and the Mosquito, and had recorded two kills. The six-foot-two pilot's résumé, dashing appearance, and thoughtful manner immediately endeared him to the other volunteers. Many non-Jews in the IAF were suspected of being mercenaries and the suspicion grew so strong that during the first truce the air force decided to largely discontinue the recruitment of Gentiles. Fitchett, though, was a special case.

No one who met him doubted his motives. In fact, a rumor started that the former RCAF pilot was the son of a minister, a Christian Zionist from birth. Though the story was not true, his desire to help the Jews was no less authentic. The seeds had been planted by a visit at the end of World War II to a German concentration camp, an experience that affected him deeply. In the summer of 1948, while in his last year of college at the University of British Columbia, he was contacted by John McElroy, a double ace who was one of the RCAF's leading fighter pilots of World War II. McElroy was recruiting for the Israelis and Fitchett was immediately receptive to the idea of joining the IAF. However, like other volunteers—indeed, perhaps even more than the Jewish ones—Fitchett had worried about his family's reaction to his decision to fly for Israel.

Like Stan, Fitchett decided to take a single family member into his confidence before heading out to war. In his case, it had been his sister Ethel, the oldest of the four Fitchett children. The two had always been close. One morning during the summer of 1948, Ethel was home playing the piano when Fitchett walked in. Swearing her to secrecy, he told her that he had decided to go to Palestine to join the new Jewish air force. She tried to talk him out of it, heartbroken at the thought of her brother, who had already spent three years in the RCAF, returning to war. He told her about his visit to the concentration camp and explained his determination to "help the Jews get their homeland back."

At the end of August, Fitchett left Canada on a four-day trip that took him through England, Switzerland, and Rome, before landing in Tel Aviv on the next to last day of the month. Less than two weeks later, he was flying for the IAF, reacquainting himself with the Mosquito and Dakota. By late September, the Canadian was commanding "B" Flight, the 103rd's new Beaufighter group.

Almost overnight, Fitchett found himself fully integrated into the IAF. His rise had been both swift and smooth. Outside of the squadron, things had also gone his way. At the end of World War II, he had fretted over the news of so many of the girls from his hometown becoming engaged while he had been away at war, fearing that he might have missed his chance. In Israel, however, he found the woman he was looking for. Ursula had immigrated to Palestine as a young girl from Düsseldorf in 1938. Her father was a veteran of the British Army and she had attended an English-speaking school in Rechavia. A friend had suggested that with her fluent English, she should join the IAF as an interpreter, and that job had brought her to Ramat David. She and Fitchett met soon after he arrived at the base, and their romance blossomed at a dizzying pace. He courted Ursula gently, telling her of his hometown in Canada and sharing with her some of his favorite poems. He showed Ursula one of his own efforts at writing verse as well as the small black Bible that he carried on all of his combat missions. Within weeks, Fitchett proposed, giving her a bloodstone ring from his own finger to seal their engagement.

Now leading the pair of Beaufighters in their first combat mission for the IAF, Fitchett attacked the El-Arish field from just fifty feet off the ground. Alerted by the first bomb run of the Spitfires, the Egyptian antiaircraft crews were now prepared, and they greeted the Beaufighters with a heavy screen of flak. Racing over the target at high speed, Fitchett caught sight of an Arab lying on the ground, clutching a rifle. In a scene that seemed to play out in slow motion, the soldier rolled to get a better angle and then fired a single shot in the Beau's direction. To Fitchett's amazement, the bullet struck the left engine, knocking it out. He tried to feather the propeller, but with insufficient oil pressure, the blade started to windmill. Realizing he would never make it back to Ramat David, he turned toward the closer base at Ekron. After an uneventful landing there, he strolled to the mess hall for a quick bite while the ground crew worked on the damaged engine.

Shortly after midnight, the third and final attack wave arrived in the form of the three B-17s. Finally, the air force had struck El-Arish and done so effectively. It would hit the field twenty-six more times over the next six days, relying mostly on the Dakotas, B-17s, and C-46s. These attacks rendered the field almost completely inoperative, giving Israel air superiority over the field of battle for the first time in the war.

A few hours after the initial El-Arish raids, the Israeli ground offensive began. Troops south of the Isolation Belt burst out in the direction of the town of Beit Hanoun in the northeastern portion of the Negev, occupying a series of strongholds. The Givati Brigade attacked from the north, gaining territory between Egyptian positions at Iraq el-Manshiya and Beit Govrin on the northern Negev's main east-west road.

Having successfully paved the way for the infantry, the IAF kept up the pressure. After nightfall on October 17, two Dakotas from the 103rd left Ramat David to bomb Egyptian troop concentrations at Fallujah, another northern Negev position astride the Majdal-Beit Govrin road. One of the pilots was

Danny Cravitt, a highly decorated U.S. Army Air Force veteran who had completed fifty-two missions over Europe in a B-24. Cravitt had not given any consideration to flying for the Jews until one day in the summer of 1948 when a friend suggested it to him in the cafeteria at the University of Florida. Intrigued, Cravitt investigated further and before long found himself in Israel, assigned to the 103 Squadron.

Sitting to Cravitt's right, in the copilot's seat, was Stan Andrews, still grounded and with no right to be on the mission. With the 103rd slated for a key role in Yoav, Stan decided he would no longer accept being kept out of the air. If he couldn't serve as a pilot, he would at least go as a crewman. He simply asked Cravitt for permission to ride along, bypassing channels that might have led back to Dr. Miller. Stan was not the first airman to joyride on a mission. Others had done the same thing, reflecting the informality that still permeated the new air force.

It was a medium-altitude affair, the kind that Stan had so disliked during his training days in the B-25. They dropped their bombs from seven thousand feet, following an approach that was intended to protect the Dakota from fighter interception. The slow-moving Dakota, pressed into service as a makeshift, medium-altitude aircraft, was not what Stan had in mind for his return to combat. His sights were on the Beau and its daring, ground-level strafing tactics that he knew as well as anyone in the IAF. Stan approached Fitchett about the possibility of tagging along on missions and he readily agreed. Stan hoped to increase his familiarity with the Beaufighter, to be ready to move into the left-hand seat when he finally received the green light to return to flying status.

Two days later, Stan and Fitchett went up together for the first time in another of a flurry of Israeli attacks against the Egyptians in the Negev. It marked Stan's return to low-altitude bombing, even if only as a crewman. Safely back at Ramat David, Fitchett sat for a debriefing. Intelligence typed it up and circulated copies throughout the IAF, including one to operations. It was the kind of close cooperation that Judah had insisted upon at the outset of Yoav.

When the report reached Judah's desk, one detail stood out. Stan's presence violated a grounding order. Of greater concern, though, was the fact that the low-altitude, daytime missions in the Beau were perhaps the most dangerous the IAF flew, something Fitchett had already demonstrated by losing an engine in his low-altitude attack on El-Arish. A B-17, Dakota, or C-46 that bombed from medium or high altitude in darkness was fairly safe from ground fire, but the Beaufighters were often within the full view and effective range of enemy gunners and were thus completely exposed, with only the speed and surprise of their attacks providing some protection. That was risk enough, but carrying a second pilot unnecessarily exposed an additional member of the IAF.

Judah was also familiar with the cockpit of the Beaufighter, and he knew there was no seat for a third crewman. An extra flyer crouched behind the pilot might well interfere with the orderly evacuation of the plane in the event of a bailout or crash. He issued an immediate order to Baron Wiseberg, the Ramat David base commander, and to Danny Rosin, the 103rd Squadron's commanding officer, to prohibit any second pilots on Beaufighter flights. That, he believed, would solve the problem.

Wiseberg had already tried to stop Stan from tagging along on missions without success. Wiseberg thought such activities were reckless and, he believed, a reaction to the stress of Bob's disappearance. As always when his mind was set on something, however, Stan was stubborn. He had come to the country to fly and he refused to restrict himself to ground duty. Judah's new order, however, would prevent Wiseberg from continuing to turn a blind eye to Stan's unauthorized flying.

But Judah's order had not made its way to Ramat David yet, and Stan wasn't finished. Following the mission with Fitchett, Stan squeezed in two more with Cravitt, one late in the night of October 19 and another before dawn on the morning of October 20. Both went off without a hitch. With the truce imminent, the afternoon of October 20 would present the Squadron with the opportunity to participate in an attack against one of the most important targets of the entire Negev campaign and Stan was determined to be a part of it.

Chapter Twenty-Two

DAY OF BATTLE

Far I hear the bugle blow
To call me where I would not go,
And the guns begin the song,
'Soldier, fly or stay for long.'"

"Comrade, if to turn and fly
Made a soldier never die,
Fly I would, for who would not?
'Tis sure no pleasure to be shot."

"But since the man that runs away
Lives to die another day,
And cowards' funerals, when they come
Are not wept so well at home.
—A. E. Housman, *A Shropshire Lad* (1896)

T
he decades-long period of British rule over Palestine was marked by frequent unrest, ultimately leading to the decision shortly after World War II to turn the fate of the territory over to the United Nations. The years between 1936 and 1939 were particularly violent. Beginning in 1936, Palestinian Arabs rose up against local British forces and the Jewish community. By the fall of 1937, the Arab campaign led to the wresting of control over a number of villages and cities, with sniping attacks and ambushes rendering many key roads unsafe for the movement of British forces or Jewish civilians. In late 1938, the Arabs of Palestine even controlled the Old City of Jerusalem for several days.

Faced with this escalating challenge, the local authorities sent for Charles Tegart, a renowned anti-terrorism expert who had made his reputation in British-controlled India, to survey the situation. Tegart's most significant recommendation called for a large number of reinforced concrete fortresses which could be defended against attack. Set on high ground, they would dominate the immediate vicinity while concentrating in one protected location all of the facilities necessary to rule: police stations, jails, courts, and government offices. Tegart believed these structures would help Britain expand its presence throughout the territory, better situating its soldiers to separate Jewish and Arab populations. Ultimately, about fifty "Tegart Fortresses" were erected.

A decade later, the fortresses remained. The one at Latrun, which loomed over the Tel Aviv-Jerusalem road, had defied repeated Israeli attacks at the beginning of the war, necessitating the construction of the Burma Road. On the Egyptian front, another of Tegart's creations had vexed the Israelis for months. Sitting astride a hilltop known as Iraq Suweidan, its commanding view of the junction of two of the Negev's main roads was critical to Egypt's control of the Isolation Belt. A maze of fences and bunkers supported by corner towers that served as lookout posts eliminated the possibility of a surprise attack.

By the time Yoav was underway, Israeli forces had attacked the fortress four times, by land and air, without success. A July mission had come closest, breaching the surrounding fences before the arrival of daylight compelled the exposed Israelis to withdraw. One frustrated Jewish soldier dubbed it the "Monster on the Hill," and the name stuck.

October 20 marked the sixth day since the start of Yoav and yet another ceasefire was scheduled for the following day. In most respects, the army's optimistic predictions had been met. A determined Israeli campaign against six Egyptian hilltop positions encircling the town of Huleikat culminated on October 19 in the opening of the Negev road. But like the Tegart fortress in Latrun, the Monster on the Hill remained a formidable obstacle, allowing the Egyptians to maintain a presence in the upper Negev. Israeli control of the desert would not be complete as long as the Monster was in Egypt's hands.

As he followed Yoav's progress, Ben-Gurion took a strong interest in the fate of the fortress. In a meeting with his commanders, he reinforced what they all knew—that its conquest would change the entire strategic situation in the south. The struggle was increasingly symbolic as well as strategic. Abba Kovner, the legendary Jewish partisan who was now attached to the Givati Brigade, wrote a poem to commemorate the struggle to take the Monster, which he described as a "fortress of sin and punishment."

With time running short and Ben-Gurion continuing to insist on capturing the fortress, the army planned a last-ditch attack. After the IAF softened up the target with a low-altitude attack by a pair of Beaus, there would be an artillery bombardment from the nearby hilltops. Sappers would breach the outer fences and then flamethrowers would sweep a path to the fortress wall. Finally, an armored vehicle carrying heavy explosives would blow an opening in the reinforced concrete, clearing the way for a final assault on the interior.

At midday on October 20, the men of the 103rd gathered for a briefing by Ernie Esakof, Ramat David's chief operations officer and another American volunteer. Fitchett and his navigator Dov Sugarman were there, as were Squadron CO Danny Rosin and navigator Sid Kentridge, who together would crew the second Beaufighter. Stan showed up as well. Esakof explained that the pair of planes would approach from the west with the setting sun at their backs, hopefully preserving some element of surprise despite the daylight hour. As the acknowledged Beaufighter expert, Fitchett would lead the raid.

That morning, word of Judah's impending order barring extra crewmen had reached Ramat David and Esakof asked Stan what his intentions were. He replied that he would be going along on the flight. Esakof asked Stan whether he had permission to go and, with Fitchett standing by his side, Stan said "yes." Esakof had not yet seen a written order from Judah and did not give the matter additional thought.

Shortly before 5 p.m., the crews headed to their planes. Rosin did not see Stan climb into the first Beau and had no idea that Fitchett's plane was carrying three crewmen. They took off and headed out over the Mediterranean, climbing to an altitude of four thousand feet before turning south. When Sugarman indicated that they were near Ekron, Fitchett led the planes east toward Iraq Suweidan.

Each plane carried two one-hundred-kilo bombs in the belly and seven thirty-kilo bombs mounted on the wings. The setup, rigged in Israel after the planes arrived from Czechoslovakia, was improvised. Two sets of switches had to be flipped to release all of the bombs, and the pilot could not flip both at once. Like many of the other Air Apaches, Stan had done some tinkering on the B-25 in the Pacific, and he had given some consideration to the bomb-release issue. He fashioned a switching mechanism that he thought would allow a simultaneous drop, and the ground crew installed it in Fitchett's Beau. One of Stan's motives for flying again with Fitchett was to see if the device worked. If it failed, he wanted to be there to help with a manual release.

As the fortress pulled into view, Fitchett lowered the nose of his plane, with Rosin on his wing. At about fifty feet, they leveled off. As they approached the outer wall, Fitchett fired his guns and cannons. Timing the flight of the bombs perfectly, he placed them into the courtyard. In the South African's plane, it was a different story. Rosin depressed the firing button for the cannons but nothing happened. As he tried again and again to get them to fire, he realized he was getting too close and quickly moved to release his bombs. Here as well, there was no response. Rosin looked up just in time to see that his wing was about to strike the fort's flagpole, and he broke sharply to lift the wing over the obstacle before banking to follow Fitchett, who had turned to starboard. In moments, they were clear of the fortress.

In the ragtag IAF, pilots had broad discretion over whether to attempt a second or even a third pass. Earlier that week, Rosin had made three attack runs at Fallujah when he realized that the Egyptians were not sending up any flak. As an Air Apache, Stan had occasionally made multiple runs when resistance was light enough to justify the risk. The pre-mission briefing might dictate, in great detail, how the first strike would be performed. But once clear of the target, the pilot decided whether or not the mission should continue.

The antiaircraft fire over the fortress had been anything but light on the first pass. The intensity of the enemy fire could be measured by the fact that Fitchett's Beau was now trailing smoke out of its port engine. Rosin was therefore shocked to see the lead plane complete a full turn and line up for a second approach. With no communication between the planes, Rosin had no choice but to follow.

The flak was continuous now, bursting around the two planes. That, combined with the smoke from Fitchett's earlier bomb strikes, made visibility almost zero. When Rosin broke sharply to port to dodge the flak, he lost the flight leader in the haze. He climbed and circled the target several times, scanning for Fitchett's plane. It was nowhere to be seen. With darkness approaching, Rosin headed back to base.

Soldiers at a nearby Israeli outpost had a bird's-eye view of the encounter. They watched Fitchett's Beau clear the fort after the second pass, trailing heavy smoke. As it turned north, it was losing altitude fast and quickly disappeared behind a hill in Egyptian territory. A billow of smoke left no doubt that it had crashed. A short while later, intelligence intercepted an Egyptian radio transmission that reported the downing of an Israeli plane and the sighting of two parachutes. The part about the parachutes was quickly dismissed by the IAF; the plane was flying too low for the crew to jump. Further, none of the onlookers at the outpost had seen chutes. The crash, however, clearly had occurred.

By the time Rosin made it back to Ramat David, the Air Force knew that Fitchett had been shot down. Desperate to give the downed men the best chance of survival, operations organized an emergency flight to the crash site. A Dragon Rapide left Tel Aviv shortly after 6 p.m., carrying a crew of three: Zvi Troyhertz, Smoky Simon, and Maury Mann. They took some Sten guns and ammo which Simon, who had engineered the rescue, hoped they could drop to the Beau crew. If the three airmen had made it out of the plane alive and had not yet been caught, the weapons could help them make it back. Within a half hour, the aid flight was over the crash site.

As the Rapide reached Iraq Suweidan, it was easy for the crew to locate the Beau, lying in the sand and burning furiously. Simon saw two Egyptian trucks near the wreckage, as Troyhertz shot past at one hundred feet. The plane drew small arms fire but completed three more passes, desperate for some sign that the crewmen had survived. None of the men were visible and there was no point in dropping the guns with the Egyptians already at the scene. With darkness falling, the Rapide returned to base.

The next night, Yitzhak Rabin, the head of operations for the southern region and a friend of Stan's since his days as air-ground coordination officer, sent a patrol to the crash site. Met by heavy fire, the soldiers were forced to withdraw without getting close. Two nights later, Rabin tried again and again the patrol was repelled.

The ground assault on Iraq Suweidan had proceeded as scheduled, soon after the Beaus cleared the fortress. The operation did not go smoothly, but a small force managed to reach the outer wall and blow open one of its doors. It was the first time that an attacking force had gotten that far. Only four men made the final assault and only one of them—the platoon leader—made it inside. After killing a number of Egyptians, he was wounded by a grenade and forced to retreat. In the end, this attack, like the previous ones, had failed.

Though the Monster continued to hold out, by October 29, the area around the crash site had been cleared of Egyptians. The IAF organized another small search party, two members of which, Lou Lenart and Sol Goodelman, knew Stan well. If there was a body to be identified, they would be of particular help.

It took two days and the assistance of spotting aircraft before the wreckage of the Beau was finally located. There was not much left of the plane, which had clearly burned for hours. There was still a single, packed parachute inside. The big discovery was a short distance from the wreckage. A nearly complete human skeleton lay in the sand. Nine days of exposure in the desert had denuded it of both clothing and flesh and there was nothing for Lenart or Goodelman to identify. Further investigation of the crash area turned up the burned remains of a document relating to Stan's service as IAF liaison to the U.N. truce supervisors.

There was a Bedouin encampment nearby, and several of the men were detained for questioning. None of them were at all hesitant to talk. The problem was that their stories didn't match up. Some claimed that the Egyptians had carted away two live men from the downed plane. Others said that two survivors had been shot and buried in the sand. Additional probes in the area, though, failed to turn up any bodies.

The search party collected the bones and returned to Tel Aviv. A cursory review suggested that they might belong to Fitchett or Stan, both of whom were roughly the same height. Subsequent examination led the medical examiner to conclude that the bones were those of Fitchett and he was laid to rest in Haifa on November 15. That meant that Stan was missing in action. The cloud of uncertainty into which Bob had disappeared in July had now swallowed Stan as well.

Chapter Twenty-Three

CHANGE OF STATUS

Show me a hero and I'll write you a tragedy.
—F. Scott Fitzgerald, *The Notebooks (E)* (1945)

T he Stan Andrews who crowded into the cockpit of the Beau that fall day in October was straddling two worlds. Committed to staying in Israel for the duration, he remained steadfast in his determination to find Bob and, abandoning his earlier certainty that his friend was dead, had become convinced that Bob had managed to survive the July 9 crash. At the same time, Stan knew the war was nearing its conclusion and had allowed himself to begin planning his postwar life back in the States.

He wrote Linden and Finley in Los Angeles about all of this on September 28. He shared with them the encouraging news about Bob—the captured Egyptian and his story about the transport of an Israeli pilot from Gaza to El-Arish on July 11, only two days after Bob's crash. Stan explained that it was his view, as well as that of the Israeli army's Deputy Chief of Intelligence Chaim Herzog,[18] a personal friend, that the prisoner in question was Bob. However, Stan also confided Herzog's belief that the Egyptians might have shot Bob if he had refused to give them information. This was sobering: "Bob, unfortunately, was the type that wouldn't give any information," Stan wrote.

Stan added that he had not written to the Vickmans about the leads he was following: "I don't want to raise any false hopes—and then have them shattered later." He would let Linden and Finley make their own decision about sharing the information with Bob's family. Should his friends decide to communicate with the Vickmans, who lived in the same city as the two men, he hoped that they would let them know that "I have been, and am, working my balls off on this—not because I want them to think I am a hero but because (a) I want them to know that he hasn't been forgotten + (b) because it's true. I can tell you that the Israel Army and Air Force have been extremely lethargic on this case + the only reason that anything at all has been done or that any investigation has been, or is being, or will be made is me. I have been on this just about every single day. I dug the abovementioned reports out of the dusty files after everyone had forgotten it or neglected to think that news of a pilot prisoner might interest anyone. I've bullied, begged, bored, annoyed + antagonized Army Intelligence

---

[18] Herzog retired from the Israel Defense Forces in 1962 with the rank of major general. From 1983 to 1993, he served as Israel's sixth president.

Officers, Air Force Intelligence Officers, Infantry Officers in the South, Air Force Colonels here, Red Cross officials, correspondents, UN observers, stenographers + everyone + anyone else I could find. I've probably succeeded in making an awful pest of myself, but at least I know that something had been done + will be done that wouldn't have occurred if I hadn't been obnoxious about it. And you can also tell them that I won't be home until I find out about him definitely one way or another—or if he's alive—until he's out." Stan wrote that he "might have some definite news—either good or bad—in about three weeks, at which time I will cable or write" the Vickmans. Three weeks later, almost to the day, Stan himself disappeared.

On November 9, the fortress at Iraq Suweidan was finally taken. In that last raid, a massive artillery barrage sapped the remaining will of the defenders, who had been holding out for months against air and ground assaults. When the outer wall was breached this time, the Egyptians inside surrendered without a fight. As the Israeli flag rose over the fortress, hundreds of Israeli soldiers watching from nearby hilltops shouted their approval, exalting in the defeat of the Monster.

Then, following a month of combat that ended on January 7, Israel completed its rout of Egypt's Negev forces. The armistice negotiations were conducted under the auspices of U.N. mediator Ralph Bunche, Count Bernadotte's successor. By July 1949, all fronts were quiet. After nearly a year of warfare and with six thousand dead—a staggering 1 percent of the country's population—Israel's battle for independence was finally over.

With the armistice agreements signed and the combatants poised to exchange prisoners, there was hope that Bob and Stan might yet be revealed as POWs. To the devastation of the families, no such notification arrived. Other prisoners of war did return to Israel, including Americans Bill Malpine and Curtis Fine. The two had landed their Norseman in Gaza on May 25, 1948, after a long and difficult flight from Europe, thinking they were touching down on Israeli soil. Fine had been captured immediately, while Malpine had managed to flee the scene and hide for several days before surrendering. The Egyptians had severely beaten Malpine before transferring him to Albassia prison in Cairo, a harrowing journey that left him battered and in fear for his life, saved only by the intervention of a sympathetic Egyptian officer. Many of the blows had landed on the American's lower back, causing temporary paralysis and then constant pain that continued to afflict Malpine long after his release from Egyptian custody.

Stan's efforts to probe the story of the captured Egyptian officer, Captain Abba Hafez, who told of escorting a pilot with an injured back, had caught the air force's attention, and it pushed the Red Cross to confront the Egyptians with Stan's theory that the pilot in question was Bob. Egypt reviewed the statement and reported: "The statement of Capt. HAFEZ concerns the pilot WILLIAM MALPINE who was transferred to EL ARISH and then to POW camp on 28/5/48 and was repatriated on Marsh (sic) 8/49." Israel showed the statement to Malpine, who confirmed that he was the pilot identified in the Hafez interrogation. As for Bob, Egypt reported: "Ref to the enquiry of the Jews about the pilot who was returning from EL ARISH on July 9th 1948 the plain [sic] was shot down by Egyptian A/A on this date and the plain [sic] and pilot were completely burnt [sic] South of Gaza near the forest and nothing could be saved." No information was forthcoming about the other two crewmen on the Beaufighter. With no alternative, the IAF changed Stan's and Bob's status from "missing" to "missing, presumed dead."

In his last letter to Linden and Finley, in which he had explained about the search for Bob, Stan had also touched on lighter matters, realizing that the war would soon be over. He kidded Linden about his decision to attend medical school: "I thought a bullshitter like you would be more interested in something like law. That's what I would have picked for you anyway. Oh well—you have my blessing, which, I'm sure, is all you've been waiting for." He proposed rooming with the two of them when he returned and mentioned that he had a chance at a Guggenheim Fellowship, courtesy of Tom Van Dycke, a correspondent who reported on the Arab-Israeli war for the *Los Angeles Daily News*. A friend from Stan's days as Andre Stanek, Van Dycke had written a strong letter of recommendation on his behalf. But whether the fellowship came through or not, Stan was sure of one thing. He was going to write a book.

The closest that Stan would ever come to writing about his last mission was a remarkably prescient essay he had composed while at UCLA. In it, he envisioned a scene very much like the October 20 raid in a story that explored the "no atheists in foxholes" theme that so intrigued him. The main character in "Milk Run" is a B-25 pilot named Captain Seymour, based in the Philippines. An officer comes to his tent to tell the captain that he needs to take a repaired plane out for a noncombat check flight, carrying a crew of two. Seymour is a cocky flyer and he persuades the other crewmen to let him head over to a portion of Manila that is still controlled by the Japanese so they can fire their ammo at real targets.

They locate the battle zone from the smoke overhead and wheel into position for a strafing run. The B-25 roars over the city with its twelve machine guns blazing, the cockpit filling with the acrid smoke of spent rounds. Unsatisfied, Seymour makes a second pass, but this time the plane is hit. He is able to set the B-25 down safely, but now the men are stranded behind Japanese lines. They race from the wreckage to find cover and plan their next move. Like Stan in the Negev, Seymour is on the ground because of two voluntary decisions—the one to fly into battle in the first place, contrary to orders, and the one to make a second pass over a hot target.

The flyers know that, if captured, they can expect to be murdered by the Japanese. Seymour is scared. He assumes they will need to fight when the enemy comes and wonders whether he should save the last bullet from his .45 to take his own life.

Seymour apologizes to the other crewmen for having gotten them into this. Then, thinking through the situation further, he has a realization. He is glad of one thing, he tells them. He had always heard that there are "no atheists in foxholes" and now he has found himself in an airman's approximation of one. Seymour had never liked that expression, explaining to his comrades: "I always thought that anyone who never did any praying until he was in a tight spot, was just a sniveling coward, with no self-respect or sustenance, turning to the supernatural because his own guts couldn't pull him through." Unlike the real story, "Milk Run" has a happy ending, with the entire crew reaching the safety of an American base. The protagonist's atheism, as well, remains intact. One can only wonder whether Stan's did too.

Chapter Twenty-Four

AFTERMATH

Saul and Jonathan,
Beloved and cherished,
Never parted
In life or in death!
They were swifter than eagles,
They were stronger than lions!
—2 Samuel 1:23[19]

B y November, the time had come to notify the families of the Beaufighter crew. The notification process for foreign volunteers had not improved since Bob's disappearance. The lack of professionalism or sensitivity on Israel's part was compounded by the fact that Stan's family had only just learned where he was and what he was doing.

---

[19]   JPS Hebrew-English Tanakh (Second Edition).

A month after the crash, the Aneksteins received a two-sentence letter, telling them that their son was missing after a mission over Egypt. It left them reeling and desperate for more information. Maybe, they thought, there was a chance that Stan was still alive. His older sister Esther took charge of things, demanding information from an Israeli government that seemed entirely deaf to her pleas. To her devastation over Stan's disappearance was now added the intense pain at being ignored by the government that had sent him into harm's way. Infuriated by the lack of assistance, she approached the U.S. State Department as well, trying to find someone who could help. She knew that Stan had survived two crashes during World War II and could only hope that he had done it again. Stan was not the only talented writer in the family and his older sister let the Israeli government know just what she thought of the treatment the family had received.

> About a year ago in April, my youngest brother,
> Stanley Andrews, a boy of 24, left our country;
> one that he loved and was proud of, to fight
> in your cause because, as a Jew, he could not
> stand by and not help. He left behind him a
> loving family and friends, an art career, two
> degrees and much that he prized.
>
> My brother flew for Israel, and then in
> November, on the 29th, came a printed letter
> of two lines, stating that he was missing since
> October 20th. Since then, not one word has
> been forthcoming from Israel. My brother was

an intimate in Dr. Weizman's[20] [sic] home, so I wrote to him. I never had the courtesy of a reply. We wired you, the Defense Ministry, with a prepared reply, and no answer. Here in the U.S., in desperation, we contacted all the people who were working in your cause—no reply; not even a word that anyone was trying to get information. Then, although knowing my brother had left his country without revealing what he intended to do, I still appealed to our president. Actually, I had no claim on courtesy from my government; but here, and here only did I receive any acknowledgment. Through all this time, only they have been making inquiries in our behalf.

The Israel Government must hold a young man's life in small regard—even less the heartbreak and despair of his family. My father glowed with fervor always about the land and hopes your country is fighting for. Now he never mentions the Jewish homeland because not only has he given a son in your cause but

---

[20] Dr. Chaim Weizmann, the venerable Zionist leader who had been a driving force behind Britain's Balfour Declaration (which was, in fact, in the form of a letter from Lord Balfour to Weizmann), was serving at the time as Israel's first president. His nephew, Ezer, was a squadron-mate of Stan's in the 101st. In an October 13 letter to the Aneksteins, Stan mentioned that he had gotten to know most of the extended Weizmann family and had been a dinner guest at the house of Chaim's brother (Ezer's father) on Rosh Hashanah, the Jewish New Year.

you have cheapened his great gift by ignoring his need of some word from you.

I know Israel is at war. I know, too, how difficult life and living must be there now. But think you, that we, who have supported and worked for your cause, don't deserve the common courtesies of the living?

Believe me, it cost many nights of grieving and trying to understand this complete indifference before I brought myself to this measure. But my parents are slowly dying of heartbreak and hoping against hope. Added to their grief is this terrible hurt that Israel, every Jew's great hope, can be so indifferent to its debts.

As a family, we are proud that we are Jews, and that you are winning your great battle, but, we are father, mother, brother and sister to a boy we loved with all our hearts.

We have lost him to your cause, but you take our gift too lightly.

As the reality sank in that Stan was not coming back, the Aneksteins now worked to at least secure the return of his writings and photos. Here, as well, they encountered baffling and frustrating inactivity on the part of the Israeli government. Air force intelligence required the photos and movie film, and these, the family was told, would not be released. As for Stan's other property, the consulate in New York finally advised Esther that it would be sent. A short while later, the Aneksteins were dismayed to receive only a pair of cloth wings.

There followed more inquiries from the family and more desultory responses by the government. By 1951, the Aneksteins had given up. It seemed that the contents of the box that Stan and Bob had so carefully packed in those hopeful days in the spring of 1948 had disappeared as surely as the two pilots had.

Not everyone within Israel was deaf to the Aneksteins' pleas for more information. After the war, Lou Lenart visited Joseph and Rebecca to share what he knew about Stan's disappearance and to express his condolences personally. Lenart had been enraged at reports that local Arabs had murdered the Beaufighter crew after the crash, and for a time even thought about leading his own raid on a nearby Bedouin encampment, using an armed jeep to unleash retribution for the murder of his friend. This was not the time for such talk, however, and Lenart listened as a weeping Joseph, clutching the picture of Stan that had won the beautiful baby contest, spoke of his son. Afterward, Lenart urged the air force to have someone of suitable stature, such as the prime minister or president, write to the Aneksteins to properly express the nation's appreciation and condolences. In 1953, on the eve of Israel's fifth Independence Day, Israeli President Yitzhak Ben-Zvi sent such a letter to the Aneksteins.

Stan's brother Is took the loss particularly hard, haunted by the fact that he alone had known of Stan's intention of going to Israel to fight and had given his blessing to the fateful plan. Is's wife had been pregnant when Stan had left for Israel and Is was determined to name the new baby Stanley. When his wife delivered a girl, he was initially undeterred. He finally changed his mind, though still insisted that baby Nerissa be given Stanley as a middle name.

Is left Stan's paintings on his walls, along with a World War II photo of his brother in dress uniform, looking like a movie version of what a pilot should be. Yet Is rarely spoke of him either to his daughter or to his son Rick, born a few years after Nerissa. Though they grew up admiring the works of art and intrigued by the handsome airman who had created them, they knew little about the person their uncle had been. Rick eventually became an artist and often wondered how his life might have been different if his talented uncle had been a part of it. One day, Is finally told Nerissa about his last meeting with Stan in New York. Is was a father who rarely showed emotion, but he cried as he relived his failed effort to keep his brother from fighting in the war that ultimately cost him his life.

After months of fruitless efforts spearheaded by Elsie Vickman to obtain more information from the U.S. State Department, Bob's family reconciled themselves to his loss, drawing even closer together. When Israel began an effort to memorialize all of the fallen flyers, the Vickman family sent a number of Bob's works, a short bio, and even a note from one of Bob's high school teachers. In 1961, Mordecai and Elsie Vickman traveled to Israel, as guests of the government, to finally see the country for which Bob had given his life.

Over the years, the Fitchetts developed a warm relationship with the local Jewish community in their hometown of Victoria, British Columbia, even donating some of Len's possessions for a synagogue display. In 1989, his older sister Ethel flew to Israel for a two-week visit. She stayed with Ursula, who returned the bloodstone engagement ring Len gave her forty years before. Ethel visited her brother's gravesite in Haifa, pressing into her travel diary a sprig of rosemary she picked there. At a party held in her honor, she met many of her brother's former squadron-mates and was moved to hear how highly they had all regarded the handsome young Canadian who had blazed such a dazzling trail through the IAF in his short time in the country. At the suggestion of one of her new friends, Ethel agreed to travel down to Iraq Suweidan, now an Israeli army base, though she had to steel herself for the journey. She pressed a flower she picked there as well, in the end, glad that she had made the trip.

For nearly sixty years, Ethel kept to herself the story of Len's visit to her in 1948 to tell her of his intention to go to Israel to help the Jews get their state. Her younger brother Roy had suspected that she had known but it had been too painful a subject to bring up. When Jeff tracked Roy down in 2005, Roy mentioned his suspicion and suggested that Jeff ask Ethel directly. She would, Roy believed, be forthcoming. Jeff spoke to Ethel three days later and she related the story of that fateful day that she was home playing the piano when Len came by to tell of his plan to go to Israel to help the Jews get their state.

Ursula, Len's girlfriend in Israel and very briefly his fiancée, was still living in Tel Aviv when we were doing our research. Ethel and Ursula had stayed in touch for many years but Ethel no longer had a current phone number. She did, however, have a last name, and Jeff was able to locate her through directory assistance. He arranged to meet her for coffee in a local café. Ursula had a bright smile, an easy laugh, and was delighted to share her memories of Len—his love of poetry (he had once written several stanzas for her), his practice of always flying with a small black Bible, and his desire to bring her to Canada after the war. It had taken her years to recover from his death and she had not married until 1957. She had three children and was now a devoted grandmother, though one could still clearly discern the lively young translator who had experienced a whirlwind romance with a dashing bomber pilot some six decades earlier.

Canadian fighter ace George Beurling, who Stan and Bob had befriended on the flight from New York to Paris, was laid to rest in Rome shortly after his death in May 1948. Two years later, he and his Jewish copilot were flown to Israel for reburial in the military cemetery at Haifa. Today, the Falcon of Malta lies just a few feet from his fellow countryman, Len Fitchett, whose body was the only one recovered from Stan's final, fateful flight.

As the war drew to a close, Ben-Gurion's attention turned to bringing to Israel the remains of Theodor Herzl, the founder of modern Zionism. It was something that Herzl himself, eternally confident that the state he envisioned would eventually come into being, had requested in his will. The interment was to be a major event for the young country, with the carefully choreographed ceremony expected to draw thousands. Colonel Baruch Komarov, Stan's army counterpart for their shared liaison work, was appointed the army's representative for the planning of the operation, which took place in August of 1949. Ben-Gurion chose a hilltop in West Jerusalem for the burial site, soon renamed Mount Herzl, and also to become the country's national cemetery. In 2004, Israel added to Mount Herzl the Garden of the Missing in Action, as a tribute to soldiers whose burial places are unknown. Its features include a series of empty graves with memorial stones for each of the missing, mostly from the War of Independence. One of those memorial stones belongs to Stan Andrews and another to his good friend Bob Vickman, symbolically reunited in the national cemetery of the state they helped create.

Chapter Twenty-Five

BIRTH OF
AN AIR FORCE

*In order to assure an adequate national defense, it
is necessary—and sufficient—to be in a position in
case of war to conquer the command of the air.*
—Giulio Douhet, *The Command of the Air* (1921)

By the end of September, with Israel's victory in sight in no small part because of the air force, Stan took a moment to savor it all. As he told his parents in the letter in which he revealed that he was in Tel Aviv: "In a lot of ways, it is very inspiring—and very satisfying, too, to see the things that Jews, who have been scorned for ages, have accomplished here. I'll tell you frankly, I am very proud to have been among them."

As Stan wrote these words, the Israeli Air Force he had come to know so well bore no resemblance to the virtually nonexistent air service the country went to war with only months earlier. On May 14, 1948, the day the government declared independence, Israel did not have a single combat aircraft and all its fighter pilots were in Europe. Having started from scratch, the IAF now boasted a squadron of frontline fighters and an all-star cast of WWII-era pilots. Added to that were heavy and medium bomber squadrons, an air transport arm, and even a dive-bombing squadron.

Today the Israeli Air Force is pilot-for-pilot one of the best in the world—if not *the* best. The qualities that make it so— rigorous training, superior dogfighting skills, audacity, and a commitment to the latest technology—were first on display during the War of Independence. The very determination to recruit foreign veterans with World War II experience was by no means preordained. Israel could have relied on the few local pilots who already had pilot training, whether military or civilian, and certainly the Arabs for their part engaged in little foreign recruitment, despite their own lack of combat-experienced flyers. By focusing on veterans, and increasingly over the course of the war on men with stellar war records, Israel ensured that it would have the best-trained and most experienced pilots in the entire theater.

The swaggering pilots of the 101 Squadron, adorned with red baseball caps sporting Stan and Bob's Angel of Death logo, represented the elite among Israel's War of Independence soldiers. They were few in number, highly and uniquely trained, and they disproportionately impacted the course of the war. While postwar Israeli fighter pilots learned to avoid the eyebrow-raising antics of the Western volunteers, they remain at the pinnacle of the Israeli military. Long after the volunteers had gone home, Ezer Weizman, who rose to become commander of the air force, continued to foster the flow of the most talented recruits into the ranks of the IAF, popularizing the slogan *HaTovim L'Tayas* ("The Best for Flying"). He could not resist embellishing it in a way that would have made his friend Stan Andrews smile: *HaTovim L'Tayas v'haTovot l'Tayasim* ("The Best [Men] for Flying and the Best Women for the Pilots").

While everyone from Ben-Gurion on down agreed that the IAF would initially rely on foreign volunteers, there was also a determination from the very beginning to train Israelis to eventually take over all pilot roles. Stan had been approached about becoming an instructor as far back as the first truce when it appeared the fighting was already over. George Lichter, one of the other American volunteers, spent a significant part of the war in Czechoslovakia training young Israeli recruits on the Messerschmitt. Two of Lichter's students (IAF Commander Motti Hod and Chief Test Pilot Danny Shapira) played pivotal roles in the 1967 Six-Day War, a war in which the IAF virtually guaranteed an Israeli victory with a dazzling preemptive strike against the Egyptian air force. That strike had been a profoundly successful implementation of the strategy first tried in the failed July 1948 raid on the Egyptian airfield at El-Arish and later, with greater effectiveness, on the first day of Operation Yoav in October of 1948.

Dogfighting excellence has been another IAF hallmark. Since 1948, more than forty-five Israeli pilots have achieved "ace" status, and an Israeli triple ace has the most kills of any pilot in the jet age. The focus on air-to-air combat had its genesis in the 101 Squadron's performance during the War of

Independence. Though the effort to bring Buzz Beurling to Israel ended with his fiery crash in Rome, other volunteers with aerial victories on their wartime resumes—men like John McElroy (ten kills) and Chris Magee (nine kills)—were able to join the 101st. The two leading aces of the war with four kills each were Rudy Augarten, an American, and John Doyle, a Canadian, both of whom had distinguished WWII records. By war's end, the 101 Squadron had recorded thirty-six confirmed kills against not a single confirmed loss in air-to-air combat.

At the onset of hostilities, the IAF could not safeguard its own air space, but within a few months the Royal Egyptian Air Force had been completely driven off, and all the climactic air battles occurred near the Egyptian border, far from Israel's cities. A July 1948 B-17 raid on Cairo was a particularly dramatic example of the expanding reach of the IAF. Israeli pilots have been bringing the fight to the enemy ever since. Even in the dark days of the 1973 Yom Kippur War, as the IAF struggled to regain its confidence after suffering devastating losses to Arab surface-to-air missiles, it kept its country's population centers safe from air attacks. At the same time, the IAF has shown, time and again, that there is virtually nowhere in the Middle East beyond its reach. In 1981, it destroyed a nuclear reactor in Iraq. Four years later, it struck the Palestine Liberation Organization's headquarters in Tunisia. And in September 2007 it hit a nuclear site in Syria. The IAF's range was most significantly on display during the 1976 transport of commandos to a dramatic rescue of nearly one hundred Israeli hijack victims, some two thousand miles away at Entebbe Airport in Uganda.

At the beginning of the War of Independence, the IAF was content to rely on the only fighter plane it could find, the highly unreliable Czech Messerschmitt. Even as Israel survived the initial invasion and successfully deployed the Me-109 to halt the Egyptian ground advance in the south, the air force continued to look for ways to upgrade its arsenal of planes. That included not just the smuggling of the three American B-17s, the only heavy bombers in use by any of the warring parties, and later the four Bristol Beaufighters, but also the replacement in September of the Me-109 with the British-made Spitfire.

With the U.S. continuing to refuse to arm Israel in the years following the War of Independence, France initially filled the breach, beginning to sell weapons to Israel in 1953. By the late 1950s, it was supplying the IAF with the Mirage, one of the most sophisticated jet fighters in the world. The France-Israel military relationship continued for fourteen years, until the eve of the Six-Day War. Still, Israel longed for American fighters and, when France ended its patronage in 1967, that longing became acute. The Haganah's pre-war plan to construct an air force based on U.S. planes finally began to achieve fruition in 1968, with the purchase of the F-4 Phantom. The U.S.-Israeli military relationship has grown by leaps and bounds since then, and, since 1980, the mainstay of the IAF's fighter force has been the F-16 Eagle. In 2016, Israel became the first non-NATO country to take shipment of the latest American fighter—the F-35.

The spirit of Stan Andrews lives on in today's IAF. Among its fighter squadrons, there is still a 101st, and it continues to proudly fly its missions emblazoned with Stan's Angel of Death logo.

Chapter Twenty-Six

THE SEARCH FOR STAN

Once there was a man who deep in his soul felt the need to be a Jew. His material circumstances were satisfactory enough. He was making an adequate living and was fortunate enough to have a vocation in which he could create according to the impulses of his heart. You see, he was an artist. He had long ceased to trouble his head about his Jewish origin or about the faith of his fathers, when the age-old hatred re-asserted itself under a fashionable slogan. Like many others, our man, too, believed that this movement would soon subside. But instead of getting better, it got worse. Although he was not personally affected by them, the attacks pained him anew each time. Gradually his soul became one bleeding wound.
—Theodor Herzl, "The Menorah" (1897)

n the late 1990s, when we first discovered Stan, the mystery was never whether he had survived his adventure. We knew from the beginning that he had not returned from the attack on Iraq Suweidan. For us, the questions focused on who Stan actually was, why he went to Israel, and what he did while he was there.

As the search began, and unaware of Esther's failed efforts to secure the return of Stan's materials—essentially the contents of the box that Stan had described in his letter to Is—it seemed that it would all be straightforward. Though we did not know specifically about the existence of a box, we knew from others in the squadron that Stan wrote often while in Israel. We reasoned that whatever he had been writing must have survived the war and made it back to the family. Once we found Stan's family, we assumed, we surely would also find Stan's materials, and with these would be able to understand and then tell his full story.

For years the testing of that theory was impossible, as we struggled with the first part of that strategy—just locating Stan's family. In researching *I Am My Brother's Keeper*, we had not needed to do any significant tracking down of individual volunteers based on our own investigative skills and instincts. We had started with some initial introductions and then invariably everyone we interviewed provided other names for us to contact. Progress was surprisingly easy and from a couple of initial interviews our total grew to over one hundred within less than a year.

But Stan's family had not been part of that network. Stan had not survived and thus had not been around to maintain contact. His family, as well, had never been part of the veteran community or made connections with any of the individuals we interviewed. In short, no one knew who Stan's family was, where they might live, or how to contact them.

Tracking them down on our own was a years long process. It began with Stan's last name—Andrews—which we were unaware was not the name he had been born with. His choice of that name had certainly changed him, as he pondered military service in the Second World War, from someone who was obviously Jewish to just another soldier with a common American last name. More than sixty years later, it also made it impossible to track his family down through name searches on the internet.

We heard rumors about Stan's family during our research for *I Am My Brother's Keeper*—that Stan was from New Jersey and that he had a younger brother who went to medical school with the proceeds of a death benefit paid by the Israeli government. We began the search armed only with that. Though the rumors all proved to be wrong, they were useful in the end. A letter to the editor of a New Jersey Jewish newspaper, looking for any relatives or friends of Stan Andrews, an American who had flown for the Israeli Air Force in 1948, led us to Joseph Jacobson, who had known Stan in high school and college.

Jacobson told us that after high school, Stan had changed his last name from Anekstein to Andrews. That was the first real breakthrough. The name Anekstein proved far more searchable than Andrews. An internet search revealed that there were only about a dozen phone listings for the name Anekstein in the entire country. We concentrated on the ones in New York, where we knew from Jacobson that Stan had lived before World War II. One of our first calls led us to David Anekstein, a distant cousin. Even though his family had long since lost touch with Stan's, David was able to give us the names of Stan's siblings (Irving and Esther) and parents

(Rebecca and Joseph). He also thought the family had moved to Los Angeles after the war.

Although not on the internet list, it occurred to us to try directory information in Los Angeles for Irving Anekstein. At the time of our call, he would have been in his eighties. We found a listing and called the number. The voice at the other end was that of Libby Anekstein, Is's wife and Stan's sister-in-law, who told us that her husband had died within the past year and confirmed that we had found Stan's family. She gave us some of her memories about Stan and immediately suggested that we call Stan's older sister Esther Hoch. Despite her ninety-three years, Esther was a tremendous resource. Her memories of Stan were vivid and expressed in a kind and articulate manner. Esther had lost nothing over the years, including both her deep sense of loss over the death of her beloved younger brother and her frustration at the treatment given to the family by Israel after Stan disappeared.

Between them, Libby and Esther preserved wonderful examples of Stan's art as well as essays he had written in high school, college, and during the interwar years. Libby's daughter Nerissa also had a large number of her Uncle Stan's stories, including "To All Concerned" and "Milk Run." Reading "Milk Run" for the first time, we immediately recognized and were moved by the obvious parallels between its central incident and Stan's real-life final mission. Perhaps the greatest prize of all was Libby's revelation to us of Stan's momentous letter to Is in April 1948, explaining the decision to go to Israel. As Craig read it aloud, it was as if Stan had stepped out of one of his photographs to speak to us directly, intent on making sure we understood his reasons for leaving the comforts of California to return to war.

Those first conversations led us in many productive directions—first among them, to Herb Linden and Gerry Findley, who had corresponded with Stan from 1945 until three weeks before his fateful October 20 mission. Each had preserved Stan's letters, which drew us even deeper into his state of mind in the final three years of his life. A particularly prized find was a letter to Linden in which Stan explained his decision to volunteer, largely, though not entirely, mirroring the one he wrote to his brother Is. Those letters were extraordinary Zionist manifestoes, all the more so coming from a writer who professed to not "give a damn about Zionism."

The letters to Is and Linden, which we discovered six decades after they were written, were like the turning on of a light in a dark room, illuminating what had been on Stan's mind at the time that he decided to go to Palestine. At the same time, they also reflected so much of Stan's voice and personality. They authentically articulated his passion on the issue of anti-Semitism in a way that the fictionalized "To All Concerned," or for that matter Stan's other writing class essays, were not fully able to do. They were also examples of Stan's biting wit as well as expressions of his deep conviction that he had figured something out that others (in this case Linden and Is) had not. The Stan who corresponded in the spring of 1948 had a strong voice—that of a wounded, driven, certain, yet also light-hearted man at a critical turning point in his life.

Linden and Findley told us about Stan's girlfriend Virginia, whom they had met and been immensely taken with. Unfortunately, neither had stayed in touch with her after the loss of

Stan. Stan's last letter to them included her street address in San Antonio but, frustratingly, not her last name, and neither friend could remember it. We became obsessed with finding her or her family if it turned out she was no longer alive. Perhaps no one would have been closer to Stan during this period of his life, and thus more aware of his inner turmoil. The street Virginia had lived on had not existed since the early 1950s, which stymied our efforts to perform some type of property record search that might have yielded the family name. For a long time, we simply accepted the idea that we would never locate her.

As a reflection of how deeply the search to uncover Stan's story had penetrated the subconscious, Jeff had a dream that the letter to Linden and Findley had actually included Virginia's phone number. Of course, it did not, but it did motivate us to try one last time to find Stan's former girlfriend. Additional searching led to the San Antonio Genealogical and Historical Society, which had records from 1948 that showed that Virginia's last name was Carvel and that she had a brother named George. A search for a George Carvel revealed two who were currently living in Texas. The first one Jeff called turned out to be a relative of Virginia's, though not her brother. He informed Jeff that she had passed away in the 1980s but gave Jeff the email address for her daughter Jenifer, who he thought would be interested in speaking with us. Jeff wrote to Jenifer, explaining the nature of our project, and referencing the oil portrait Stan had painted, surmising that Jenifer might be familiar with it. She had heard of Stan and was delighted to talk, filling in many of the gaps of our knowledge about Virginia. We learned that the original of the painting is lovingly displayed by the oldest of Virginia's five children, while the others have digital copies. Jenifer shared with Jeff an electronic version as well as a photograph of her mother during her service in the WAVES. Virginia had been a loving mother, revered by her children, and Jenifer asked Jeff to promise that in writing about her mother, he would always be respectful—an unnecessary request that itself said much about Virginia and the kind of person she had been.

As we expanded our search outward from the protective circle of Stan's family and closest friends, we also located high school and college classmates and nearly a dozen of his World War II squadron-mates and even attended an Air Apache reunion. We renewed our acquaintances with surviving members of the 101 Squadron, who we had interviewed for *Brother's Keeper*, and located several more that we had not been able to question previously. They all added significantly to our picture of Stan's experiences in Czechoslovakia and Israel.

We met with Smoky Simon, the air force officer who was on the plane that flew low over Stan's burning Beaufighter soon after the crash, hoping to drop weapons to the crew. He shared his original logbook entry for the flight, including his detailed observations of the crash scene. We also talked to Sol Goodelman, Walter Firestone, and Lou Lenart, members of the search party that found the wrecked plane in late October, and Amit Shrem, the air force historian who identified the rediscovered wreckage in the 1990s.

The location of Stan's personal possessions has proven far more elusive. Early in our conversations with Esther, we realized that Stan's writings from his time in Israel had never been returned to the family. With the letter to Is, we now knew more specifically that there certainly should have been something substantial, but we also knew there would be no easy way, or perhaps any way, to track them down. Over time we clearly found some things that had been in the "box." At the main Israel Defense Forces' archive in Givatayim, we found a file marked "*Izvonot* Stan Andrews" ("Stan Andrews' estate"). Inside were some gems—detailed, handwritten essays on his first mission with the 101st and his ruminations on the loss of Bob. There were also a significant number of his typewritten memos from his time as the air force liaison to the U.N., shining a light on this chapter of his service. There must have been a good deal more—putting to one side the photographs and movies, we suspected that there were multiple notebooks with handwritten entries, perhaps typewritten pages as well, and sketches. Stan wasn't a diarist—Bob was and we located two of the diaries he kept (one in WWII and one in Israel)—so we do not believe there would have been a diary in the traditional sense. We believe instead that he composed individual essays on notable events, like his first fighter mission and Bob's disappearance. In Stan's letter to Linden and Findley at the time of the first truce, he wrote: "So far as the book is concerned, I've collected some terrific material but it's background + preparatory stuff." In his last letter to his friends, months later and after he had been through so much, he again declared his intention of writing a book about his experiences, this time not including any concern about a lack of material.

Over the years, we have constructed theory after theory about what may have happened to the remaining contents of the box and who may have ended up with them, and over time have pursued them, one after another, with no luck.

After quickly realizing from our conversations with Libby and Esther that the materials had not been returned to the family, the next most logical place to look was Israel's official military archive at Givatayim. That search initially netted us the *Izvonot* Stan Andrews file, but not much else. We discussed the matter at some length with Major Avi Cohen, IAF, (Ret.), the former head of the historical branch of the Israeli Air Force and the leading expert on the early history of the IAF. Though retired from all military service, Cohen volunteered for nine days of reserve duty and thoroughly scoured the archive, in a way that only someone who knew it intimately could. His search yielded a trove of additional material, including Mordecai Vickman's last letter to Bob; memos regarding the identification of the body found near the wreckage of the Beaufighter; and dazzling photographs of the Monster on the Hill, nearly all of the key players, and even of the Beaufighter burning after the crash-landing in the desert. However, he did not find any more of Stan's own writings or drawings.

We searched other archives as well, among them the Central Zionist Archives in Jerusalem, the American Machal archive in New York, and the IAF Museum in Beersheba. We encountered no success at any of these either.

We considered whether the Vickmans, rather than the Aneksteins, may have somehow been sent the materials, and perhaps not spoken with the other family about them. Esther told us during our first conversation that she believed the Vickmans had blamed Stan for Bob's death, assuming that Stan had been the driving force behind the friends' joint decision to volunteer. She said, without bitterness, that she fully understood why they may have felt that way. However, our conversations with the Vickman brothers, both Harry and Ted, made it clear that the Vickmans also had not been sent any materials from Stan and Bob's box.

We also speculated that Ezer Weizman may have ended up with them, based on a tantalizing memo from 1949, sent while Weizman was the commander of the Ramat David air base. In it, Weizman reported that he had custody of Stan's possessions and asked for direction on where to send them. We wondered whether that direction may never have come and whether he may have simply held on to them for safekeeping, knowing that they had been meaningful to his friend. He may have also been aware of the depth of Esther's anger and been concerned that if the materials were returned to her, they could have been shared with the press, which might have led to the leaking of military secrets. We asked Weizman's widow about the possibility that he may have Stan's writings. Early on in the conversation, she told us how much Weizman had loved the squadron, its men, and its logo. The first time she met Weizman, he had been driving a car that the squadron had stolen and then marked with Stan and Bob's Angel of Death logo. But she had never seen anything resembling Stan's materials in Weizman's possession.

Beyond that our theories became more far-fetched. We looked into whether Baron Wiseberg, Stan and Bob's friend from training in Czechoslovakia and Stan's squadron commander in the 103 Squadron, might have ended up with the materials. He would have uniquely understood the value of what they were creating and would have cared that they not be discarded. In 2015, we tracked down his nephew Adam. Wiseberg had passed away some years before and Adam provided some wonderful color about his uncle. But the contents of the box had not ended up with his uncle either.

Another theory, and one that has been difficult to test, was that they had been misrouted to the family of a different deceased soldier. The basis for this one came from a mix-up that involved, of all people, the Vickman and Fitchett families. In 1950, the Vickmans finally received back from Israel several suitcases containing Bob's clothes. Inexplicably, Len Fitchett's wallet was among the items they found inside. Wanting to return the wallet but not knowing who to send it to, Elsie enclosed it in an envelope addressed to Fitchett. In an accompanying note, she explained: "Our son Robert Vickman was killed on July 19 - 1948 (sic) in Palestine. Some of his things were sent home and among them there was some papers and a wallet belonging to Leonard Fitchett. I have mailed them to the address I found. Please let me hear from you of Leonard. I addressed them in his name as I don't know if he has a family."

Undoubtedly there are other possibilities. Perhaps they never made it into the archives in the first place or were removed for some reason after having been delivered. Perhaps they were misfiled and have eluded our discovery for that reason. The list goes on.

It is of course entirely possible, if not probable, that the remaining materials were simply thrown away or destroyed somewhere along the way. On this possibility, we reasoned that there was nothing to be gained by theorizing how the materials may have been discarded. If, in fact, that happened, we simply would never find them. However, we have always believed that anyone who came into possession of a series of notebooks and sketchpads, filled with creative content about an epic event in Israel's history, would never have purposefully destroyed them.

Beyond that practical surmise, there has always lurked a mystic belief that has driven this book from the beginning. The power of Stan's personality has left us with the overwhelming sense that his was a story that was meant to be told. The twists and turns that we have encountered along the way— finding the letters to Is and to Linden where Stan explained his decision to volunteer, locating Virginia's family as a result of a dream, reading "Milk Run" with its nearly prophetic foretelling of Stan's last mission—have made us feel not just that this is a story that must be shared, but also that the materials needed to tell it would ultimately be found if we just looked hard enough and continued to have faith. That belief has been strengthened by our discovery of Stan's own determination to write a book about his experiences. We would like to believe that, in some measure and particularly through liberal quotation from his essays and letters, we helped him achieve a literary ambition that he held dear.

At the same time, we have realized that so much of the richness of what we learned about Stan came from the personal recollections of family, friends, and squadron-mates; the yearbooks he worked on in high school and college; the Air Apaches memory book; the letters from World War II, the interwar years, and Israel; the essays from high school and college—all things that would never have been in the box that he built with Bob. Not having the luxury of being handed at the beginning whatever it might have contained, we have been forced to take the long way around, a path that ultimately led us to a richer and broader set of insights into who Stan was and what drove him forward, and that has given us what we needed to tell his story. We still hope to one day find more because Stan's story has always been so compelling to us and the idea of one day reading more of his own words—biting, sarcastic, funny, passionate—remains tantalizing. Perhaps, with the publication of this book, they will yet come to light. Until that day we must remain, to borrow from *Ethics of the Fathers*, happy with our lot.[21]

For the two of us, who have felt the deepest calling to tell Stan's story, there have been countless surprises, coincidences, and lucky breaks along this journey—serendipitous moments that have made the entire experience intensely meaningful. Unlike with *Brother's Keeper*, the research for this book, like Stan's journey, was not straightforward. Yet it was never dull, never exhausting, and indeed it is more in sorrow than in joy that we greet its completion. Stan made the fight against anti-Semitism and the struggle for a Jewish state the defining causes of his life. In many ways, telling his story has been the defining cause of ours.

---

[21] "Who is the rich one? He who is happy with his lot...." Pirkei Avot (*Ethics of the Father*), 4(1).

Chapter Twenty-Seven

REFLECTIONS

*Those who today inaugurate this movement are unlikely
to live to see its glorious culmination. But the very
inauguration is enough to inspire in them a high pride
and the joy of an inner liberation of their existence.*
—Theodor Herzl, *The Jewish State* (1896)

I n 1948, Stan Andrews found himself forced to confront
powerful questions of Jewish identity in the wake of the
Holocaust, in an America in which anti-Semitism remained
commonplace, and at the dawn of the rebirth of a Jewish homeland in the Land of Israel. Those questions were visceral then.
The Holocaust was an open wound, the extent of its horrors
far from fully known. Anti-Semitism of the variety that Stan
encountered in the army was impossible to avoid, even if physically nonthreatening. And most significant, there was great
doubt as to whether a Jewish state would succeed in emerging

from the chaos following Britain's departure from Palestine, in the face of local Arab violence and a threatened invasion by all neighboring Arab states.

Stan's response to all of this was to decide that he could not remain indifferent, despite his ambivalence about his Jewish identity. In a sense, he had it all in 1948. He had started a new life in sunny, bustling, Los Angeles. He was studying on the GI Bill on an idyllic university campus. He had a beautiful, talented, devoted girlfriend—adored by all who met her. And, as always in his life, he had a circle of close and admiring friends. For nearly anyone else in his situation, anxious to make up for time sacrificed for military service, it would have been more than enough. For Stan, it was not.

It is not difficult to imagine what Stan's life would have looked like had he stayed in California. He would have finished his master's degree and found his footing in some way professionally, perhaps even in the movie industry that had so stimulated his excitement before the move to Los Angeles. Once he had found his niche, his many talents and personal gifts would have ensured ever-increasing career success. He no doubt would have overcome his commitment phobia, married Virginia, and raised a family, creating a satisfying postwar life that became the lot of the overwhelming majority of his contemporaries. Yet he chose differently, and for that he is a figure of immense interest and inspiration to us.

Though the issues are less immediate, in a way the conflict between a quiet American life and a resolution of the Israel question remains for many the classic American Jewish dilemma. For those American Jews, like us, who have had the good fortune to be born in the second half of the twentieth century or later, life in this country is overwhelmingly good. The doors of all of the most prestigious universities and workplaces have been thrown wide open. Jews are fully integrated socially and, indeed, intermarriage and assimilation are far greater threats to American Jewish survival than hatred.

And yet, below the surface, things are perhaps not as different as we would like to believe. Anti-Semitism remains a feature of American life. On the far right, hate groups are vocal, organized, and occasionally militant. The 2018 Pittsburgh synagogue shooting—an event unlike anything experienced by the American Jewish community in Stan's day—has shown that the physical threat they represent is real. Though the Trump administration provided enthusiastic and unqualified diplomatic and military support to Israel, its dog whistle politics—including loaded rhetoric about left-wing, financially powerful Jews like George Soros and the principals of Goldman Sachs—have given hope to the haters of the right that their views are entering the mainstream and becoming ascendant. Perhaps nowhere was that more pronounced than Donald Trump's stunning characterization as "good people" marchers in a neo-Nazi rally in Charleston, South Carolina, in 2017, many of whom were wearing Klan or Nazi paraphernalia and chanting slogans like "Jews will not replace us." Though little commented on, the fact that Trump's "America First" slogan is the same one that Charles Lindbergh used in his Jew-baiting campaign to keep the U.S. out of World War II raises uncomfortable associations with past hatreds.

The left side of the political spectrum increasingly gives vent to its own demons where Jews are concerned. For them, it is supposedly about "Zionism" and Jewish "settlements." These are the things they claim to abhor, while usually proclaiming a lack of animosity for Jews as individuals—despite rising numbers of physical attacks against Jews and synagogues in the name of protesting Israel. The left's *cause célèbre* has been Boycott, Divestment, Sanctions (BDS), a Palestinian-Arab-founded group that has gained increasing traction on university campuses and within liberal political circles, and which seeks to entirely delegitimize the Jewish claim to Israel. Effectively, it seeks to reverse the outcome of the 1948 and 1967 wars, throwing Israel back from all "occupied" Arab territory and returning the descendants of the Palestinian Arabs who in 1948 fled their homes in Israel. The group Black Lives Matter (BLM), which exploded into prominence following the George Floyd demonstrations in the summer of 2020, has enthusiastically endorsed Palestinian claims, seeing opposition to Israel as an extension of the fight against white racism. This view is gaining increasing influence within the Democratic party generally, particularly among a new generation of politicians and activists who see the world through a racial prism and to whom the Arabs are the authentic and eternal residents of the region—people of color who have been ousted by a Zionist movement led by white, European, Jews.

For American Jews, there is a need to choose politically between a party that is home to both passionate supporters of Israel and classic anti-Semites versus one that has long enjoyed majority Jewish support but that is increasingly identified with relentless criticism of the Jewish state and indeed a questioning of its very right to exist. It is a terrible dilemma, at least for those for whom both Jewish and Israeli survival are dearly held values.

However, for most American Jews, having achieved acceptance and belonging, Israel is an increasingly distant and irrelevant issue. Israel has become, like Zionism was in the years before World War II, an issue that does not stir great interest or passion. In an America that no longer insists on reminding us that we are different, we can forget that we were born Jewish and simply get on with our lives, something that Stan tried to do before he joined the Army Air Corps. We can ignore both Israel and BDS. For those Jews who subscribe to the Zionist vision of a Jewish homeland but who do not see life in Israel as a desired or practical possibility, we can today be loyal Americans and passionate supporters of Israel and not fear the charge of dual loyalty. Or, as many on the left have now found appealing, we can swing from a reflexive defense of our coreligionists in Israel—a legacy of the post-WWII outpouring of support for the struggle for a Jewish state that swept up Stan more than seventy years ago—and now sympathize with, or even vigorously support, the aims of BDS. All options are on the table.

Yet whether or not American Jews want to acknowledge it, and though certainly the balance of power has shifted, Jews in Israel remain under siege. The country has been in a state of war every day of its existence since May 14, 1948, a couple of weeks before Stan arrived in the country. When we were doing the research for *Brother's Keeper* in 1996, we met Marlin Levin, who had moved from Philadelphia to Palestine in 1946 with his new bride, where both served during the War of Independence. Sitting in the living room of his Jerusalem apartment with his wife by his side, he told us with amusement how their American friends had cautioned them in 1946 that things were dangerous in Palestine and they should wait for the situation to calm down before going. "Had we taken that advice," Levin said, "we'd still be waiting."

Israel has fought conventional wars with neighboring Arab countries in 1948, 1956, 1967, and 1973. There have been multiple conflicts with Lebanon since 1982, where a Hezbollah-led government continues to stockpile rockets for yet another massive barrage on Israel, one that could break out literally at any moment. Fighting with Syria has flared from time to time since the first Lebanon war, continuing to this very day. Palestinian terrorism has been uninterrupted since Israel's founding, gaining increased organization and intensity since the founding of the Palestine Liberation Organization in 1964 and through a series of intifadas in the 1990s and early 2000s where the image of the suicide bomber stepping onto an Israeli bus or entering an Israel café became seared, at least in the Jewish consciousness. Since Israel's withdrawal from Gaza in 2005, it faces essentially a second rocket-armed Lebanon in the south, where several major campaigns (most recently in 2021) have failed to eliminate the threat posed by a Hamas regime armed with rockets that can reach nearly every corner of Israel. Indeed, the Israelis are the only residents of a developed country, anywhere in the world, that make regular use of bomb shelters. Meanwhile, a nuclear-ambitious Iran hovers on the periphery, providing military assistance in Lebanon, Syria, and Gaza and vowing to wipe Israel off the map.

American Jews can avert their eyes from all of this or try to convince themselves that it is all Israel's fault and therefore unworthy of their concern. Indifference to what is going on in Israel is certainly an option, but it is not an inspiring one. As Stan Andrews discovered in 1948, it is difficult, no matter how assimilated we become and how comfortable we might be, to ever really be aloof from questions of Jewish identity and survival. After 1948, wrestling with such questions includes a need to come to terms with the State of Israel.

In the two thousand years before Israel's founding, Jewish exile was marked by all manner of rejection and violence, including expulsions, pogroms, and crusades, culminating in the Holocaust. The last of these—not just the German mass murder of one out of every three Jews alive in the world at that time but also the collaboration or indifference of virtually every other country—showed once and for all that Jewish security can never be taken for granted in a world that seems always to find a reason to return to ancient hatreds where Jews are concerned. It is a lesson too easily forgotten.

And yet, the American Jewish coming-to-terms with Israel does not have to be only about accepting the need for statehood as the ultimate guarantor of Jewish survival. It can be about recognizing, and in some way becoming part of, an inspiring journey that shows over and over again the heights to which human determination can take us. The Jewish return to statehood after two thousand years of exile and only three years after the devastation of the Holocaust, the revival of the Hebrew language (something even the greatest of visionaries Theodor Herzl thought impossible), and the ingathering of exiles from every corner of the world—the vision and audacity of it all—have no historic parallel. Winston Churchill captured it perfectly in a speech in the House of Commons in 1949, calling Israel's creation: "[a]n event in world history to be viewed in the perspective, not of a generation or a century, but in the perspective of a thousand, two thousand or even three thousand years." Stan was able to take stock of the remarkable history playing out before him, writing the month before his last mission of his pride in having been part of it.

The Jews of Israel have not just survived in the face of unrelenting wars over the last seven decades. The country has modernized, accepted waves of immigration (from the Arab countries in the 1950s, the former Soviet Union in the 1980s, and Ethiopia from 1984 to 1991) that no other country would countenance much less embrace, and become an admired center of technology, science, and entrepreneurship. Israeli disaster-relief teams are on the scene for earthquakes and tsunamis around the world, at least in those countries that will have them. Israeli development assistance flows to more than half a dozen African countries. It has become the "Start-up Nation," one of the greatest incubators of technological innovation in the entire world. That is not to say that Israel is without flaws. Conflicts between religious and secular, those who serve in the army and those who do not, the economic haves and have-nots, Israeli Arabs and Israeli Jews, the settler community and those who seek territorial compromise—are serious and real. In many ways, though, those flaws make the accomplishments all the more impressive.

None of this was inevitable when Stan arrived in the back of a C-46 in the spring of 1948. The struggle for independence could have succeeded and then Israel could have become an irrelevance to the rest of the world, an indistinct country that fails to inspire, that lacks audacity, that contributes little or nothing outside of its borders. Most countries fit that description and there is no shame in that; certainly, Israel could have joined their ranks. And yet that drive to become something distinct, special, and inspiring was always there, whether in the religious ideal of Israel serving as a light to the nations or Herzl's vision of a Jewish state that would become a center of culture, cure malaria, and help develop Africa.

Herzl's vision of Jewish statehood was still only that when the War of Independence began in May of 1948. A Jewish victory was far from assured as a lightly armed and hastily organized Israel Defense Forces faced a multipronged invasion on all fronts. As had been the case during the Holocaust, the rest of the world looked on with little more than indifference at what could have been another Jewish calamity, with only Czechoslovakia, in the end, selling weapons to the Jews. The war was inexplicable in the face of what today is seen as political orthodoxy for resolving the Arab-Israel conflict—the Palestinian Arabs of 1948 were in their homes, a Palestinian Arab state was poised to be created alongside a Jewish one, and Jerusalem was to be an international city. Yet the notion that there would be a Jewish state of any size was unacceptable to the Palestinian Arabs, whose leadership had successfully demanded a closing of Palestine's doors to Jewish immigration following the rise of Hitler, when millions sought to flee the Nazis.[22] There has been no internal Arab reassessment of the political leaders of the 1948 period, no questioning why they

---

[22] Hajj Amin al-Husayni, the grand mufti of Jerusalem and the leader of the Palestinian Arabs from 1921 until after the War of Independence, made common cause with the Nazi regime. In 1941, he traveled to Berlin to meet with Adolf Hitler, telling the führer that the Arabs were Germany's natural friends because they had the same enemies as Germany—the English, the Jews, and the Communists. The mufti pledged his support for the German war effort and later recruited Bosnian Muslims to the SS.

chose war when the Palestinians already had or were poised to receive all that they claim to want today. Rather, the War of Independence remains in Arab eyes "al-Nakba"—the catastrophe. It is a telling characterization and one that, until replaced with a sincere reassessment of the 1948 Arab rejection of partition, suggests that true peace will remain a long way off.

If the need for war in 1948 is difficult to discern when viewed through the lens of current political discourse, it is impossible to understand given the landscape that remained after the 1949 armistice agreements with Egypt, Jordan, Syria, and Lebanon that ended the fighting. Once the 1948 war ended, the Arabs occupied every inch of the West Bank, Gaza Strip, Golan Heights, and East Jerusalem. Yet there was no movement to create a Palestinian Arab state within these territories, and instead Arab claims focused only on what they did not have—control over that portion of Mandatory Palestine occupied by Israel. As with the leaders of 1948, Palestinian and regional Arab leaders of the 1949–1967 period have never been the subject of any critical reexamination for their failure to establish a Palestinian Arab state in the postwar, Arab-controlled lands that ostensibly represent the entirety of Arab territorial claims against Israel.

For those who are burdened by concerns over Jewish settlements and current Israeli security practices and who are sympathetic to the argument that a return to the pre-1967 borders will solve everything, Stan's experience is a reminder of what that world looked like. The reality of Israel's formative years—a full-throated Arab rejection of the partitioning of Palestine into Jewish and Arab states living side-by-side—is a challenge to the conception that the conflict today can be fully explained, much less solved, by an exclusive focus on post-1967 events. What happened to Stan is far more than an interesting footnote to a major historic event. It clarifies fundamental questions of Jewish survival, Palestinian intentions, and peace—questions that were relevant when they thrust themselves into Stan's thriving postwar life and that remain so today.

Moving beyond historical context and deeper political meaning, Stan's story is that of a single individual reacting in a surprising and bold way to a series of dramatic events affecting the Jewish people, to whose ranks he only nominally and uncomfortably belonged. There were ample reservoirs of sympathy for the Zionist cause among American Jews, especially veterans, in the years following the Holocaust. But only a small number, less than one thousand of the more than five hundred thousand Jews who served during World War II, actually went to Palestine/Israel to fight. If one had to predict which American Jews were least likely to go, Stan, no doubt, would have been near the top of any such list—his flight from Jewish identity and belonging seemingly complete by the spring of 1948. Yet he went.

For Stan, it all began as an amusing adventure filled with intrigue, international travel, a chance meeting with a beauty queen, fighter pilot training behind the Iron Curtain, a dramatic nighttime landing in a plane filled with smuggled weapons, and a successful mission at the controls of a Messerschmitt. Had the fighting ended in June after the first truce, it would surely have been an amusing story to tell—a summer of lighthearted adventure. "Did I ever tell you about the time that I was a fighter pilot in the Israeli Air Force?" Stan might later have told his kids, or, as he had written his brother about speeches he might one day give, "I flew planes for the Haganah!"

The July 9 raid that claimed Bob challenged Stan, a second time. In coming to Israel, he had decided to grasp hold of the chance, as a Jew, to stand up and fight back—in the process walking away from a girlfriend for whom he cared deeply and interrupting the arc of his postwar life at a time when other veterans were determined to make up for time lost during WWII. While the first part of the experience had been raucous and amusing but without any real cost, everything was different after Bob's disappearance and the Radio Cairo report that he had been killed. At that point, Stan had a perfect opportunity to walk away from it all, just another volunteer who had given enough and who had had enough. But he would not do that and also would not shrink from his original decision to stand and fight, in a literal sense, against those he saw as the enemies of the Jewish people.

At every turn, it seemed that Stan's story had involved irony. It began with the most assimilated of Jews traveling to Israel to fight. He had made that trip with the taciturn Bob Vickman, an unlikely yet extraordinarily close friend. It was there again with the Beaufighter. The Beau was one of the very planes that as Andre Stanek, Stan had been trying to shield from U.N. inspectors. After the loss of his liaison position, the Beau would become his coveted destination within the air force, a return to bombers/strafers. A key role in enabling that return was Len Fitchett. The Canadian was a friend very much in the Bob Vickman mold—thoughtful, serious, and also an unexpected volunteer for the Jewish cause.

And perhaps the final irony was the sharing of Bob's fate. The two friends had made the decision to volunteer together, they had traveled together, they had trained together, they had arrived together, they joined the same squadron, they designed its logo, and in the end in missions occurring months apart, they shared the same mysterious fate.

The things that moved us when we first "met" Stan Andrews move us still: his decision, as a highly assimilated Jew, to fight for a Jewish state; his and Bob's audacious plan to record the war; his unrealized talent and ambition; and his unresolved disappearance. The survival of Stan's Jewish identity despite all the factors that seemed to be working so successfully to subvert it was, in the end, perhaps no less surprising—or inspiring—than the survival of the painted Jewish star on the burned and desert-exposed wreckage of the plane that had carried him to his destiny five decades earlier.

In his March 1948 letter to Herb Linden, Stan wrote: "When these guys get through, when you hear the word Jew mentioned you'll think of something else besides a pawn-broker or shopkeeper." That prediction has been realized, in spades. To his eternal credit, he helped make it so.

Note About the Chapter Quotations

Each chapter is introduced by a quotation from a book, poem, speech, film, or magazine article. We selected only those that could have been read (or heard) by someone living when the events described here took place. Some held particular meaning for one of the men in this book. The World War II expression that there are "no atheists in foxholes," in Chapter Eight, was the one that Stan explored in "Milk Run." Len Fitchett was fond of "High Flight," which introduces Chapter Twenty-One and Fitchett himself into the story. Fitchett identified "Day of Battle," which introduces Chapter Twenty-Two, as one of his favorites in a book of poetry he sent to his brother, and it speaks with the same prescience as "Milk Run" in foreshadowing that fateful day at Iraq Suweidan when Fitchett (with Stan crammed into the cockpit) chose to make a second pass over a hot target rather than fly away after his initial bombing run. Bob read *The Robe*, which introduces Chapter Seventeen, while serving in the Pacific. Its sentiment that there are points beyond which you cannot push a Jew captures the "fighting back" spirit that drove both Stan and Bob to go to Israel, to give their lives for a Jewish state, and to help make history.

Acknowledgments

We have benefitted from the generous assistance of many people over the years of work on this project. There are several who deserve special mention. Major Avi Cohen, Israel Air Force (ret.), is a former head of the Israel Air Force Historical Branch and the leading expert on the IAF in the War of Independence. Perhaps no one was more intimately familiar than him with the intricate organization of the archived records for this period of Israel's existence. Moved by Stan's story, Avi volunteered for nine days of reserve duty to search for Stan's missing materials, an extraordinary act of generosity that yielded a trove of additional documents that we likely never would have otherwise found.

We are especially grateful to those friends and family members of Stan's who saved his letters, essays and art—it would have been impossible to write this book without those materials, or the wonderful insights of the people who shared them with us. We include in this list Esther Hoch, Libby Anekstein, Nerissa Anekstein, Ellen Brener, Susan Winik, Harold Lachs,

Herb Linden, and Gerry Finley. Though she of course did not know Stan, we must also mention in this context Jenifer Webb, one of Virginia Carvel's children. Jenifer shared her loving memories of her mother, a digital copy of Stan's oil portrait, and a picture of her mother during her service as a WAVE.

We will always be grateful to Reuben Rosenfeld, a friend of Jeff's, who was the one who suggested that we write a letter to the editor of a New Jersey Jewish newspaper regarding our search for people who knew Stan. That led us to Joseph Jacobson, who took the time to respond to the letter and got us solidly on the right path for our research by disclosing Stan's name change—which Joseph also illustrated with copies of pages from their shared high school (Anekstein) and college (Andrews) yearbooks. In many ways, all of our later research successes began with this one suggestion by Reuben and the response by Joseph.

Jeff had the privilege of getting to know several of the men with whom Stan served as an Air Apache, including Don Wagner, Stanley Muniz, Murph Leventon, Tal Epps, Joel Newman and Syl Mawrence. They gave Jeff valuable insights into squadron life, shared with him after-action reports and photos, and in general provided a fuller sense of what it was like to serve in this dangerous and highly-decorated World War II bomb group. We add to this list Jay Stout, a prolific aviation writer and the author of *Air Apaches: The True Story of the 345th Bomb Group and its Low, Fast and Deadly Missions in World War II*, an outstanding book about the unit. Jay graciously shared with us digital copies of official archival material about the Air Apaches.

In our efforts to learn more about Stan's time in Israel, we benefitted greatly from interviews with Giddy Lichtman, Leon Frankel, Smoky Simon, Lou Lenart, Mitchell Flynt, Coleman Goldstein, Sid Cohen, Harold Livingston, Sol Goodelman, and Lee Silverman. In 2019 we were honored to meet with Dan Tolkowsky, the Deputy Chief of Operations for the IAF during the War of Independence and later the IAF's third commander—still spirited and engaged at ninety-eight. Tolkowsky described to us how he had stood in the street in Tel Aviv on May 14, 1948, where he listened to the loudspeakers blare out, live, David Ben-Gurion's speech declaring independence. In Tolkowsky's five years as the IAF's commander, he of course met with Israel's first Prime Minister often. During WWII, when Tolkowsky had initially been a student in England and later a member of the RAF, he had attended a Churchill speech—where Tolkowsky had personally experienced the rhetorical power of one of the greatest speakers of the 20th century. For those of us engaged in historical research, it does not get much more exhilarating than hearing of these personal encounters with legends of history—at the same time a reminder of just how recent all of this actually was.

In our efforts to learn more about Bob Vickman, we were extraordinarily fortunate to have been able to spend time with Harry Vickman, Bob's oldest brother. Harry shared wonderful stories about Bob, their shared childhood, and the Vickman family as it was in the 1930s and 1940s. Harry also showed us several of Bob's paintings, which we were able to photograph, and allowed us to copy Bob's WWII diary. The third Vickman brother—Ted—was also extremely gracious with his memories.

In one of our conversations with Harry, he mentioned that Bob had been extremely close with one WWII squadron-mate in particular—Dick Mischke. It took a while but we tracked down Dick who, it turned out, was an aviation legend. Dick stayed in the U.S. air force after WWII. Like Bob, Dick had also wanted to be a fighter pilot. After the war Dick was able to transfer into fighters. He flew 100 missions in Korea and, as a squadron commander, 274 in Vietnam. He retired as a full Colonel and, when Jeff was speaking with him in 2010, he remained an active pilot and instructor—one of the oldest flight instructors in the U.S. Dick was generous with his time and spoke with precision and color about his experiences in the Pacific with Bob, whom he referred to as "the best friend I ever had."

To learn more about the remarkable Len Fitchett, we were fortunate to track down Len's younger brother Roy and then, through Roy, Len's sister Ethel. Roy provided us with wonderful memories of his revered big brother Len. Roy still had the book of poetry that Len had sent him more than sixty years earlier and was able to identify the poems that Len had marked for Roy to read. Ethel shared with us the secret that she had kept for more than half a century—the tragic moment when Len had told her of his plan to go to Israel to help the Jews get back their homeland. Together, Roy and Ethel were able to share with us copies of Len's World War II and Israel logbooks, letters from the time of his service in the RCAF, photographs, a whimsical postcard that Len had sent from Europe while on the way to Israel, and even his membership card in the Caterpillar Club (whose members had all successfully "hit the silk"—bailing out of a disabled plane before it crashed, as

Len had done during WWII). Ethel also shared with us Ursula's full name, which allowed us to track her down in Tel Aviv, where, in 2009, we were able to enjoy a delightful cup of coffee together at a local café.

We were also interested in Dov Sugarman, the third crewman on the Iraq Suweidan raid. Dov had been married to Lilly, pregnant with what was to be their first child, at the time that he disappeared. It all remained an open wound for Lilly, who later remarried and raised a family but still preserved the memory of Dov. It was an extraordinary sacrifice for her to relive the shattering experience of losing her first husband.

We have continued to scour the archives in the years following Avi Cohen's 9-day search and have located numerous additional items over the years—including a full set of the memos that Stan wrote during his time as liaison to the U.N. truce supervisors, records relating to his other missions with the 103 Squadron, and documents related to the attempt to determine whether the Israeli pilot prisoner of the captured Egyptian Captain was Bob Vickman. These successes were made possible by the patient and expert assistance of the archives staff, including Limor Itzhak and Orna Zohar and by professional researcher Daniela Reiss, who was introduced to us by Limor. In this context we also wish to acknowledge Amit Shrem, who was serving in the air force and was attached to the Israel Air Force museum in Beersheba when the remains of the Beaufighter were found in the 1990s. Talking with Amit about his identification of the Beaufighter wreckage was one of the more moving episodes of the entire research effort.

We must also acknowledge Nancy Spielberg, who produced "Above and Beyond," an award-winning 2014 documentary about American volunteers in the War of Independence. Nancy shares our passion for this subject and—more than any other person—has brought the volunteer story to life for so many American Jews who would never otherwise have heard of it.

In Israel as well, the contributions of the volunteers have not been forgotten—nor the unfinished business of locating the missing and bringing them back for a proper burial. Stan Andrews and Bob Vickman are still very much on the minds of the Israel Defense Force's Missing in Action Division. A conscientious reserve officer named Baruch (not his real name) currently heads the search for their remains. Baruch was kind enough to take Craig to the precise location of the Beaufighter's final resting place—now a modern neighborhood—and to show him the path that the plane would have taken in the last moments of its flight. We are grateful for the time he gave us and hopeful that his immensely important search for Stan and Bob may yet be successful. We were also moved to learn from Baruch that he had insisted that Stan be officially listed as the first case officer assigned to the search for Bob, given all that Stan had done between July and October 1948 to find out what had happened to his missing friend.

We appreciate all those who read earlier drafts of the manuscript and who provided valuable feedback and suggestions. We include in this list Russ Roberts (who has given advice and guidance throughout the process), Tal Keinan, Gary Belsky, and Neil Fine. We could not be more grateful to the legendary editor Claire Wachtel, who transformed the book by helping us sharpen our focus on the things we should be writing about, while overcoming the classic writer's unwillingness to kill darlings. It was an extraordinary privilege to be able to work with Claire.

The team at Wicked Son has been an absolute pleasure to deal with at every step of the way—led by the remarkable Adam Bellow. Adam set a joyful tone right at the beginning, emailing Jeff to set up their first phone call with the comment that "this will be an easy conversation as I've already decided to publish your book." We were privileged to have been able to work with Aleigha Kely, who kept this project perfectly on track in a kind and tactful manner, and Aleah Taboclaon, whose copy-editing saved us from more than one obscure, yet embarrassing, factual error. (Who knew that Filipino whiskey was made from fermented palm sap and not cactus?)

In some ways this work began in 1995, the year we started our research on *I Am Brother's Keeper*, when we first discovered Stan. It became more intensely focused in 2005, when Joseph Jacobson responded to our letter to the editor in New Jersey. No doubt we have forgotten the contributions of others who have helped us over the years and for that we apologize. Writing this book has been a true labor of love for the two of us—an epic journey that only the luckiest of writers get to take. We could not be more grateful to those who lent a helping hand along the way—both those we mention here and those we may have, to our collective chagrin, forgotten. We appreciate you all.